Be A Good Boy

Cover and interior design by Tabitha Lahr

Published 2018
Printed in the United States of America
Print ISBN: 978-1-7325988-0-5
Digital ISBN: 978-1-7325988-1-2
Library of Congress Control Number: 2018910648

Be A Good Boy

My Journey from Self-Loathing to Self-Love

Robert W. Finertie

Part I

"More precious was the light in your eyes than all the roses of the world."

—Edna St. Vincent Millay

Prologue

Mom picked a lousy time to die. It was Labor Day 1941. I was eight and a half years old as I peered into the casket. We were in the Dobbins Memorial Methodist Church of Delanco, New Jersey. The woman lying there looked like my mom, her arms folded across her chest holding a white corsage. I could trace the veins in her hands, the thin blue trails that once carried life to her arms so she could hug me, to her cheeks so she could smile at me, and to her lips so she could kiss me good night. But her eyes were now closed. How I wished she would open them and look at me to reassure me of her love. Dad said she was in heaven. I'm sure he meant that to be reassuring. It was not. Heaven was a vague place somewhere up in the sky. I guess she needed her eyes up there, wherever "there" might be.

I would learn later that children up to the age of about twelve have a concrete-operational frame of reference through which they see the world. They see trees, not the forest; waves, not the ocean. During this stage of development, a child has no ability to grasp concepts or ideas. He sees Nana and Grandpa, not grandparents; cousins who play croquet on the back lawn are Cousin Dick and Cousin Fred, not sons of our parents' siblings.

I saw the locket I gave her fastened around her neck. I didn't understand. When I bought it, I'd thought it would help her get better. It hadn't.

She appeared the same as she always did, except she didn't move. She didn't breathe. She didn't look at me. That was what bothered me most of all, that she didn't look at me. I touched her hand. It felt cold. Dad asked if I wanted to kiss her good-bye. Yes, oh yes. He lifted me up so I could kiss her on her cheek. Her cheek was cold too. Yes, I wanted to kiss her and I wanted her to kiss me back. No, I didn't want to kiss her good-bye. I didn't want her to go away.

Dad put me down and said, "Don't cry. Be a big boy." The church organ played softly in the background. Art Young sang, "Softly and tenderly Jesus is calling, calling to you and to me," in his distinctive tenor voice.

The man in the black suit from the funeral home asked me if I wanted Mom's locket.

"No," I told him, "I gave that to my mommy."

As he closed the lid of the casket, I heard people sobbing. I watched Dad fighting back the tears, just after he'd told me not to cry. I wanted to cry. I wanted to rage and yell and scream, "That's my mom, and I don't want her to go away!" There was a battle going on in my head between those words and these: "Be a good boy. Don't cry."

Forty years later, this poem bubbled up from whatever deep recess I had buried it in:

The Day the Lights Went Out

"Don't cry," he said the day earth swallowed up the one who bore me.

"Don't cry, for when you do my own grief threatens to overwhelm me."

"Don't cry; for I must work so we can live, if survival counts as life."

"For the dam, once compromised by one small teardrop, would allow such torrents of anguish and despair to follow that none could stanch them."

"Don't cry," he said, and I made some vain attempt to please him,

To comply, so I would not be twice bereft.

"Don't cry"? When fate has intervened;

When death's icy fingers rend my bosom

And rip my heart—still beating—from my breast?

"Don't cry"? When from life's treasure chest

The pearl of greatest price has been removed?

"Don't cry"? When at the point of greatest need for comfort

The greatest source of comfort has been taken?

My mother

Chapter 1:

An Early Winter

The day before Mom died, Dad and I walked to the Zurbrugg Memorial Hospital in Riverside, New Jersey, so we could visit her. To get to the hospital we had to cross the Rancocas Creek, which separates Delanco from Riverside as it flows south to merge with the Delaware River. Knowing that we would cross this bridge, I had gathered a handful of pebbles along the way. Now, as we walked across it, I was tossing the pebbles into the water, enjoying the kerplunk they made as they hit the water, fascinated by the way the rings of ripples expanded as they were carried away by the current. This was a mindless pleasure that served as a brief respite from my fears about Mom.

Once we cleared the bridge we walked past the J.D. Collins Lumber Yard on our right. A few blocks farther across the street sat the Riverside Metal Company and The Keystone Watch Case Company, with its large tower and the clock that reminded residents of the time—visually with its Gothic face and acoustically with its Westminster chimes. There were strong family connections here. Grandpa had worked at Keystone for forty-two years and retired as the superintendent of the Tool Crib. Dad worked at the Metal Company for forty-five years. He would eventually retire as foreman of the Finishing Room. Later, I would work in the quality control lab for four years after graduating from high school.

After crossing the railroad tracks, we came to Main Street, downtown. Dad stopped at a jewelry store and we peered through the window at the jewelry on display before opening the door to go inside. Wouldn't I like to buy something for Mom? he asked.

There were so many items to look at, and I had no idea what I might want to get her. Patience was not one of Dad's strong suits. Before long he was shuffling his feet and jangling his house keys on the glass countertop. These two actions were probably unconscious nervousness on his part, but to me they trumpeted the "hurry up" message that was such a constant part of the background noise of my childhood, like a dripping faucet that gets increasingly annoying over time.

The sales clerk, a redheaded beauty in her late teens, wore her hair in a bun with a pencil stuck through it. After Dad explained our mission, she said, "How about

The Keystone Watch Case Company

Three generations of Finerties

one of these?" pointing to a glass shelf full of necklaces. I felt grateful for her help narrowing down my choices.

After studying the necklaces a bit, one caught my eye. It was a silver chain with a heart-shaped pendant on it. On the left side of the heart was a red gemstone. As soon as I saw it, I knew that was the one.

Dad signaled to the clerk that the price was okay, so she removed it from the case and draped it over her hand so I could get a closer look. "I'm sure your mother will love it," she said. And I knew she was right. She placed it in a gift box and tied a ribbon around it with a bow on top.

After we left the store I felt a new spring in my step as we walked the remaining three blocks to the hospital. I was with Dad. We were on our way to see Mom, and I had a beautiful gift in my hand to give her.

My brother, Ken, wasn't with us that day. He was five and a half and I was going on nine. I supposed he was too young to understand, which meant Dad thought I was old enough to understand. I wasn't, but I tried to live up to his assumption. The reality was that I would never understand. What I knew about death then wouldn't fill a thimble. What I don't know about death now would fill the Mariana Trench, an abyss in the South Pacific seven thousand feet deeper than Mount Everest is high.

As we entered the hospital, Dad had to help me with the heavy door. Once we were inside, he went to the receptionist's desk to sign in and tell them who we wanted to visit.

Dad seemed friendly with this woman with curly hair and gold-rimmed glasses. He motioned in my direction and she looked at me with a kindly smile. There was no way for me to know then that years later she would become my stepmother.

Mom was in room #247 on the surgical wing, so we took the elevator to the second floor. I wanted to see her so badly, and the elevator seemed so slow. It took forever to go up one floor. When the doors opened, the hospital smells assaulted our nostrils. Odors of living and dying, and of bodily functions that Lysol and air fresheners can't quite erase and Jean Nate After Bath Splash can only partly cancel.

When I entered the room, Mom was sitting up in bed. She smiled through her pain as I ran to her side.

"Oh Bobby, I'm so glad to see you."

"Mommy, Mommy, I brought you a present."

Excitement crackled in me as I watched her open it. She saved the bow and carefully folded the wrapping paper. She gasped as she saw the necklace and gushed, "Bobby, I love it." Will you help me put it on?"

I felt pride swelling my chest as she savored my gift, warm and fuzzy all over. "I picked it out just for you, Mommy."

"I know you did, dear, and that's what makes it so special to me."

As she spoke, I saw her tense up, a sign that spasms of pain were racking her body.

Dad picked up on it too. "We'd better go now and let your mother get some rest."

"When are you coming home, Mommy?"

"Soon, I hope," she said. She patted the bed and invited me to sit beside her. She took my hands in hers, looked at me with her warm, brown eyes, full of the love that only a mother can show, and said, "Be a good boy, Bobby," as she squeezed me. I felt so caressed by her loving gaze—so nurtured and appreciated—that I began to cry. It was a moment when none of us could speak.

As I searched Mom's eyes, I saw that alongside all that love there was something else, something not so easy to describe. Her soul was troubled by things I had no words for and she was unable to say. Be a good boy, because life will be easier that way. Be a good boy, because I am not going to be here to take care of you. Be a good boy, so your father won't have to spank you. We were all in tears as Dad and I went out the door.

I didn't know then that those five words would be her last to me. Her death later that night would make it so.

Sometime during the middle of the night after our visit to the hospital, I awoke to strange noises, like the sounds wounded animals make, coming up the stairs. Ken and I were staying at Nana's house in Riverside, New

Jersey, while Mom was in the hospital. I woke up Ken. As I opened the bedroom door, the sounds got louder. I had never heard sounds like these—high-pitched, ruptured souls wailing their cries of pain. What could cause such lamentation?

We tiptoed along the hallway to the top of the stairs. The living room was full of people. They were crying, "Oh, no." "What happened?" "I don't believe it." "God help us."

We moved cautiously down a few steps. Now we knew that something had gone horribly wrong. I flew down the remaining stairs, ran to my dad, and grabbed onto his leg as if my life depended on it. It did, but I wouldn't know that until later.

Dad unfastened me from his leg, picked me up, and held me close. I felt his body shaking uncontrollably.

"What's wrong, Daddy?" I asked.

He tried to answer but grief choked back the words.

"It's your mother," my aunt Sara answered for him. She was his younger sister.

"Where's my mommy?" I cried out. "Where is she?"

"She didn't make it," Aunt Sara said. "She died in the hospital last night."

"No, no, no!" I screamed. "Mommy, I don't want you to go. I don't want you to go. Who's going to take care of me?"

Nobody answered. They were all too busy crying and carrying on.

"Oh Reeb, oh Reeb," my dad cried out and squeezed me tighter.

Nana had her hanky to her mouth; her eyes were all rimmed in red from crying. Tears ran down her cheeks and landed on her dress. Even Grandpa was welling up. I had never seen him cry.

Aunt Sara, Uncle Ed, and Aunt Mary; Nana and Grandpa; my dad, my brother, and me—a room full of people helpless in the face of death, reduced to children mourning the loss of sister-in-law, daughter-in-law, wife, and mother.

I went away that night. That's the day the construction of Fort Heart began. "I don't ever want to hurt like this again," I told myself. From that moment, I began to build a fortress around my heart—an armored cave, a safe place where pain could not come in. I wouldn't realize this, however, until much later.

Mom's death imprinted my soul and bruised my heart with the agony of losing a loved one—along with the absolute terror of feeling abandoned.

Ken and I were expected to go back to school the following Monday. But our hearts were on a different schedule. Mom's death chilled us like the first northeaster of the season. Winter would start early that year, in September.

Chapter 2:

Nana and Grandpa's House

Ken and I had been staying with Nana and Grandpa Finertie since Mom went into the hospital. Someone had to look after us while Dad was at work. Their house was located just a few blocks from the hospital. We loved visiting them because there was a public park across the street from their house with a monster slide and a swing set. That slide was the tallest and scariest one in the area. We wore ourselves out climbing up the twelve steps and then gliding down the slide. We'd alternate seeing how high we could go on the swings and then how fast we could go down the slide.

After an hour or so of this we were tired, thirsty, or had to pee, so we returned to Nana's house. It was my job to make sure we "looked both ways before crossing the street." While we were using the bathroom we would hear the familiar sounds of Nana chipping ice for our ginger ales from the twenty-pound block of ice in the icebox. Then we'd run to the kitchen for a cold drink and a slice of pound cake. Nana always asked if we had washed our hands before she gave us our treats.

In the picture I'm holding, Nana and Grandpa are seated in the living room of their house on Carroll Street. Grandpa is on the viewer's right with his elbow resting on the arm of his favorite Morris chair. He's holding a cigarette between his thumb and forefinger, just like the movie stars, at eye level. It would have been a Chesterfield and it would have been placed, ritually and with precision, in his amber cigarette holder before he lit it. The remainder of the pack would be in his shirt pocket under his vest. Clad in a three-piece suit and tie, Grandpa sits there relaxed, with his left ankle resting on his right knee. A handkerchief folded into three points juts nattily from the pocket of his suit.

Nana and Grandpa were my paternal grandparents. Nana's name was Charlotte, but Grandpa called her Lot. His name was John Albert, after the Prince of Wales. Dad's brother, Uncle Ed, called him "Fifth Cavalry John" because of his service during the Spanish American War.

The photograph is black-and-white, now turned sepia from age. Grandpa is not looking at the camera. He never did. Instead, his eyes are focused 45 degrees to the right. His posture suggests he might be thinking,

Nana and Grandpa

Well, go ahead if you must, but I'd really rather not—except that he would never have used that many words. Grandpa lived for ninety years, painfully self-conscious of a lazy eye that seemed to have a mind of its own. As a child, I never knew which eye to look at when he spoke to me—which, thankfully, wasn't often. When he spoke, most of his dialogue was in response to a prompting from Nana: "Isn't that right, John?" "Yes, Lot."

I think Grandpa may have taken Calvin Coolidge as his model. In those days, people referred to the president as "Laconic Cal" because he rarely spoke more than two words at a time. It is reported that at one of his fund-raising dinners a heavy financial supporter asked to be seated next to him. Her aim was to win a substantial bet that she had made with one of her friends: that she could charm President Coolidge into saying something more than his usual two words. At what she believed to be an auspicious moment, she leaned toward the president and said, "Mr. President, I have wagered a substantial sum of money that I can persuade you to respond with more than a two-word answer."

The president took in her request, thought for a moment, and said, "You lose."

I feel a certain sadness that I don't know much about my grandpa. I suppose that most of the "don't talk" messages

I got as a child came from this side of the family. How I wish that I had asked more questions to draw him out. "What was it like to serve under Teddy Roosevelt and his Rough Riders?" "Were you ever involved in any bloody battles?" "Did you ever have to kill anybody?" "What do you remember best about that time of your life?" But even if I had, who knows what kind of answers I would have gotten? My hunch is that not much information would have been forthcoming (due to the "no talk" rule), and even if he had surprised me with an answer, I'm sure any future inquiries would have been parried with, "You ask too many questions."

In the photo, an ashtray sits on a stand between Nana and Grandpa. It's full of cigarette butts. Nana smiles pleasantly at the camera, her face relaxed and welcoming. She was a substantial woman, and in the photograph she's wearing a long, checkered dress that is gathered at the waist. The hankie she always carried is tucked under her belt.

Nana was the socializer of our family. She carried the bulk of the conversation. She was also fond of food, as her size attested. Whenever Ken and I visited, as we ate our slices of pound cake, she would moisten her index finger and use it to mop up the crumbs. I never saw Nana eat a slice of cake, only the crumbs. As I look at her in the picture, however, I know she must have had her share.

On Saturday afternoons back then, the Paramount Theater in Riverside featured a matinee for kids. Mom would feed us lunch and send us off to the movies. She'd take her coin purse out of her pocketbook, unsnap it, fish for a dime and a nickel, then place the coins in my outstretched hand and close my fingers over them with the reminder, "Be careful not to lose it." I was eight and Ken was five and a half; as the older brother, I was custodian of the funds. In 1939, movies cost eleven cents, and children under six were free, so with the four cents change, I'd go to the candy counter and buy a four-foot tape of sugar dots to eat during the movie.

This outing was a special treat for us, and it provided some alone together time for Mom and Dad. When the movie was over and we came out of the theater, we'd have to squint for a few seconds—the sun was so bright after being in the darkness. After our eyes got adjusted, we'd run around the corner to Nana's house, a block and a half away.

One day, Ken and I burst through the back door and found Nana sitting in the darkness at the end of the table in the dining room. She gasped in surprise—"Oh Bobby, I was just enjoying a few filberts!" She had no lower teeth in front, so she was pressing the hazel nuts against her upper teeth in the only way she had to chew them.

Nana turned crimson as her mind registered that someone had seen her without her lower teeth. In an atmosphere where perfection was a paramount virtue—preached and practiced, if not achieved—I found her humanity endearing.

During the summer, the ice man would deliver ice on Monday, Wednesday, and Friday. This was before the invention of refrigeration. The Schaefer Ice Company would provide its customers with an 8½" x 11" cardboard sign with numbers on it. On ice days, housewives would place the sign in the window so the driver could see how much ice to deliver. For example, one side of the card might read "10 & 20," and each number could be read only one way. If you wanted twenty pounds of ice that day you put the card in the window so the driver could read the "20" (the "10" would be upside down.) The delivery man would see the number and chop a twenty-pound chunk from the two-hundred-pound block in the back of his truck. He'd move the blocks of ice around with tongs that helped him get a grip. He'd hoist the twenty-pound block up onto his shoulder to carry it into the house. A thick leather apron protected his shoulder and side from the cold and the drips.

During the winter months, Nana didn't have to buy ice because she could keep things cold in a window box.

Another reason Ken and I loved to visit Nana and Grandpa is that Uncle Jack would read to us when he was there. He'd sit on the sofa, flanked on either side by the two of us, and we'd snuggle up to him as he showed us full-color pictures of birds from the dictionary and read to us about where they lived and what they liked to eat.

He told us the birds were our friends and we should call them by name, just as we do with our people friends. We were both starved for this attention, since Mom was in the hospital and Dad was away at work. We loved Uncle Jack because he found time to be with us.

Uncle Jack wasn't really our uncle; he was Nana's brother, which made him our great-uncle. But that was complicated, so we just called him Uncle Jack—and because he was English and had an accent and said "bids" for birds, we called him "Uncle Jack that says 'bids.'"

Most of our visits to Nana's house were enjoyable, but one item in their house struck terror into our young hearts. Outside the second-floor bedroom where we slept, a black cast-iron fixture hung on the wall. Its function was to hold a box of matches to light the gas lamp next to it. Nana called it Lucifer, which literally means "light-bearer." But Ken and I were not buying that explanation. In our little hearts we knew that Lucifer was much more sinister than that. He was, in fact, viewed by us as Satan in disguise, like a black Santa keeping an eye on us.

If we slept through the night, Lucifer presented no problem. He was on the outside of our bedroom and the door was closed between us. But it was troublesome when we woke up during the night and had to go to the bathroom. That trip took us down the hallway right under Lucifer.

We never made that trip alone. Even the thought of a confrontation with Lucifer in the dark scared us spitless. If I needed to get to the bathroom, I woke up my brother so we could face Lucifer as a team. Then we'd crawl along the baseboard, keeping as close to the wall as we possibly could, so he couldn't see us.

Lucifer was only one scary aspect of staying overnight at Nana's house. There was another thing that was even scarier because it wasn't a figment of our imaginations—it was real.

I remember a few times waking up during the night, startled to find someone in the bed with me. It must have been someone I knew, because I didn't feel afraid. It could have only been Uncle Jack, the one who read us bird stories and called the birds "bids." He was naked and hovering over me. He pulled down my pajama pants and I saw that he was holding his member in his hand.

"Be quiet," he whispered, "don't make a sound."

I stared up at him, terrified.

"I just want to put mine on top of yours," he said. "Is that okay?"

I sensed that saying "no" was not an option.

He aligned his member with mine. His was bigger. I felt the weight and the warmth of his body as he lowered himself on me. There was movement down there where our penises touched. It didn't hurt—in fact, it felt good—but it didn't feel right, either.

My memory of this event is such a blur that I don't

know if it only happened once, or multiple times. I do know that I never talked about it, ever, to anyone. After that night, whenever we visited Nana's house for Thanksgiving and Christmas, I got terrible migraine headaches.

Chapter 3:

The Early Years

One Monday morning in spring of 1937, the screen door slammed shut. Mom walked over to the back porch swing, set our wicker laundry basket down in front of her, and plopped heavily into the seat of the swing. She was crying.

"What's wrong, Mommy?" I asked.

She blew her nose into her hankie and wiped away her tears before speaking. "Your father left for work and he didn't put up the clothesline. Now I don't know what I'm going to do."

This is my first conscious memory. I was four and a half years old. I remember pausing to size up the situation. I could see in my young mind that Mom was too short to reach the hook that held the clothesline. An idea came into my brain: "I know, Mommy: if I lean my fire truck against the house, you can stand on it and you'll be able to reach the hook."

It seemed so simple to me, but Mom was blown away that I thought of this solution. She bragged to all the neighbors about how clever I was to figure that out. At the time I felt warm and cuddly basking in the sunshine of her praise. Later I would see it as the first step in my long journey of trying to please people so they would love me. Even later, I would wonder why Mom didn't think to get a ladder or a chair from the house to stand on.

That question puzzled me for many years. When I received the letter from Dr. Shipps, however, I began to connect the dots. This scene could have taken place about a year after my brother's birth. Mom would have been weak from loss of blood and she would have been experiencing major discomfort down below as the result of the trauma of a difficult delivery. I'm sure everything must have felt overwhelming for her during that time.

Mom and Dad had known each other for several years before they married. They lived as neighbors on Hickory Street in Delanco—the Broomes (Mom's family) at 629 and the Finerties at 623. In his distinctive hand, Dad wrote on the back of his favorite picture of Mom, the one he carried in his wallet, "Riverbank, Delanco, 1926."

Dad and Mom on the beach, 1930

The date of their wedding was June 30, 1928, according to their marriage certificate.

At times I have wondered what activities they may have enjoyed doing together. Delanco took pride in fielding semi-pro teams in basketball, baseball, and football. Dad said that Babe Ruth played there once in an exhibition game. The Volunteer Fire Company staged water fights once a month to keep their skills sharp and to entertain the townspeople. During these battles, the crowds cheered for their favorite teams. The engines of those Seagrave pump trucks roared like lions fighting for their lives. The needles on the pressure gauges trembled just below redline. The firemen directed those powerful streams at each other, sometimes tearing away pieces of clothing, until one team relented.

The Rancocas Creek and the Delaware River offered opportunities for canoeing, swimming, boating, and waterskiing. During the summer, people flocked to the shore at Atlantic City, only an hour away, to stroll on the boardwalk, swim in the ocean, eat saltwater taffy, or just bask in the sun.

During the early years of their marriage, my parents lived at home with Mom's mother, Mary Prudence, nee Brown, Broome. The 1930 US Census sheet for Hickory Street lists them as residents at 629. Mary P. Broome is listed as the head of the household, Reba, Clara, and Jessie as her daughters, and Bob as her son-in-law. Mom's older sister, Abigail, had married Ralph K. Messick in 1924 and moved to Beverly, about five miles north of Delanco.

The family worshipped at the Methodist Episcopal Church on Union Avenue. The Reverend James F. Baughton performed Mom and Dad's wedding there. They presented me for baptism at that church as well. The pastor baptized me with "water from the Jordan River," the certificate states, and my parents dedicated me, their firstborn child, to the Lord.

Dad served for years as the superintendent of the Sunday school. Mom maintained the list of newborns from the church on the Cradle Roll.

Mom's sister, Clara, married Uncle "Jack" John L. Carhart on June 28, 1930, shortly after the census was taken, and moved to Riverton, New Jersey. Her youngest sister, Jessie, continued to live at home and was still there when I was born, on October 2, 1932. She married Uncle "Jack" John H. Maloy on June 17, 1935. They bought a house in Beverly, New Jersey, and moved there.

I was four and a half, going on five years old, when Dad opened the front door and yelled, with some urgency in his voice, "Bob, come outside quick! You'll never see anything like it!"

I quit whatever I was doing and ran outdoors. I heard it before I saw it—the Hindenburg, the largest airship in the world. Its hulking gray mass, nearly three football fields long, loomed in the sky over our little township. My jaw dropped as I looked where Dad was pointing and saw the vastness of it. The Daimler-Benz engines were producing the sound I heard as they labored to push this behemoth through the sky, a massive cloth-covered envelope held aloft by more than seven million cubic feet of hydrogen gas. Dad and I kept gawking at the sky even after she was gone, wanting to see more, hoping she would come back, knowing that we had just witnessed something special. Like my mom, she didn't stay long enough with us; she went away too soon, and she was never coming back.

Later, we learned that the airship had been circling the area around Lakehurst, New Jersey, for nearly two hours, waiting for severe thunderstorms to pass and for the winds to calm enough for landing. Delanco was only thirty-five miles west of Lakehurst. We didn't know then that Dad's statement would become prophetic; neither we nor anyone else would ever see anything like it again, because at seven fifteen that evening, the Hindenburg, airship LZ-129, burst into flames. The fire, stoked and superheated by all that hydrogen, reduced the hulking airship to a tangled mass of smoking aluminum girders in less than twenty minutes.

Only the people of Lakehurst knew about the tragedy at first. The next day, radio station WLS in Chicago broadcast an audio tape recording made by their correspondent, Herbert Morrison, who was on the scene at Lakehurst covering the historic landing. Emotion choked the announcer's voice. At times he could not speak as he watched the mighty airship go up in flames and tried to describe the horror that he was witnessing.

British Pathé Films got some footage of the scene and did a voiceover using Mr. Morrison's recorded commentary. In those days, the only way you could hear the news was by huddling around the radio in the living room. We had a Philco. To see the news you had to go to the local movie theater. Once there, you watched the previews of coming attractions and the Pathé newsreel or the Movietone News, teasers before the screening of the featured film.

The next day, Uncle Ralph drove us all over to Lakehurst in his '36 Buick so we could see the wreckage firsthand. But Lakehurst was a naval air station, and the military police had cordoned off the area. So we were able to view the scene only from a great distance, which was totally disappointing after having seen her aloft over Delanco.

Chapter 4:

Learning Shame

The black plastic nozzle was attached to a red rubber hose that led to the bottom of a hot water bottle that hung from the shower. That image woke me from a sound sleep and stirred up a six-pack of emotions. It was a flashback to my youth, from when I was four or five years old. I felt anger, fear, rage, anxiety, loss, and shame all at the same time. Anger because I was being attacked, assaulted, invaded, and penetrated by my mom and dad. Not by an enemy—I would expect harsh treatment at the hands of an enemy—but by Mom and Dad, people who were supposed to love me. I didn't expect it from them.

I felt anxiety because they had done it before. It was like the second time you jump out of a plane with a parachute. The first time, you don't know what to expect. The second time, you do. I knew that we were going into the bathroom. I knew that I would have to take off all my clothes and climb into the bathtub. I knew that I was going to be held down against my will. I knew that they wouldn't listen to my protests. I knew that resistance was futile. They were stronger than me. They were going to put that black plastic tip up my butt. They were going to release that warm, soapy water out of the bag until it was all inside me, and I felt like I was going to burst. I was being raped by my parents. I was being forcibly violated and penetrated by a foreign object at the hands of my caregivers. *Why are they doing this to me?* I wondered. *When will this stop? Will it ever stop?*

I felt rage because I was so helpless. It didn't matter what I wanted or didn't want because they were stronger. Two grown adults against one child—I didn't have a chance. No matter what I said or did, I was powerless to prevent it. I begged them to stop. I yelled, "Stop doing this to me!" I struggled, I twisted, I kicked. Nothing worked. I tried to bite them and got whacked on the butt. I got so tired that I couldn't fight anymore.

As soon as I relaxed, they stuck that plastic nozzle up my butt. It went inside my body. I felt the warm water as it ran into my body. There was too much. I couldn't hold it all. My stomach hurt, bad. I thought it was going to bust. Then everything came out, in a hurry, all at once and all over the place. I don't remember what happened after that. I think this was when I first learned to go away.

I didn't know what to call the feeling I was experiencing then. Today, I know it was shame.

I felt that there was something wrong with me. Why couldn't I poop like other people did? What was wrong with me that my body couldn't do what normal bodies did? Why couldn't I do it myself? I heard other kids say, "Look, Mommy, I did it myself." Later, when I tried to help my own children, they would often say, "I want to do it myself, Daddy." And I let them, of course.

Later I learned that this was called "autonomy," and that's why I'd felt ashamed all those years earlier—because my parents had taken away my autonomy. I think my cousin, Dicky, was struggling with the same issue, because one afternoon shortly afterward, we both reclaimed our autonomy: we pulled down our pants and shorts, sat on the second-story windowsills, let our butts hang over, and pooped on the roof below.

We got our autonomy back after that, but it cost us dearly. Somebody got punished that day—but I didn't feel it, because once again, I went away.

I don't know how long the enemas continued. I felt afraid they would never end. I do know that it was an experience I dreaded. Something I didn't want. So I learned to go away. I escaped to a place in the corner of the ceiling where I could observe what was being done to little Bobby without feeling the pain.

Later, I wondered how the enema thing even got started in the first place. Was I having trouble going? Was I trying to hold on? Was this a contest of wills between my parents and me? Was it a health issue, or a fad of the times, or a medical recommendation? Somebody mentioned that John Harvey Kellogg, MD—of cereal renown and head of the Battle Creek Sanitarium—believed that most illnesses originated in the stomach and bowels and counseled daily yogurt enemas to produce sparkling clean intestines. Perhaps my parents had picked up on this and wanted the best for me . . . but at what cost? Clearly, they weren't picking up the emotional cues, weren't seeing that during these sessions I basically willed myself to disappear.

John Harvey Kellogg

Chapter 5:

The Rules

Not all memories of 629 Hickory Street are painful. Dad built a sandbox in the backyard. It was one of my favorite places to play. I spent hours building sand castles, moving sand around with my front-end loader, hauling it in my toy dump truck, and watching, fascinated, as the granules of sand passed through a sieve.

My top choice of backyard activities was playing in a tub of water. On summer days, Mom would fill a round galvanized washtub with cold water in the morning and we'd wait for the sun to warm it. There were no hot water heaters then. If you wanted hot water, you put water in a pot and heated it on one of the burners of the gas stove.

Mom would fix us some lunch and then insist I take a nap. After that she'd put on my bathing suit, or not, and

I'd run outside to frolic in that tub with rubber duckies and a toy tugboat. She'd provide a paintbrush and a pail of water and I'd paint the back porch or the side of the house. I used a corncob pipe and a cake of Ivory soap for blowing bubbles, an activity that still brings me joy. These household items offered hours of fun with no cost of admission.

Those were the years following the Great Depression. Money was scarce. Dad had a decent job, yet he made only $7.50 in exchange for a week of his life, Monday through Friday plus a half-day on Saturday.

In July of 1938, I was sitting with my brother at the table in the dining room eating supper. I was five and a half, he was two. We always ate fast so we could go outside to play before it got dark. There wasn't much conversation, but there was a lot of tension. It was not a comfortable place to be. Yet one of the house rules demanded that we stay at the table until "your daddy has finished eating." Another rule was, "Take as much as you want and eat as much as you take." If we ever took more than we could hold, another rule demanded that we "sit at the table until we could hold it."

I was sitting at the table, staring at my plate. The meatloaf was gone, because meatloaf was my favorite. There was some residue from the mac 'n' cheese and a purple spot where the beets had been. The source of the tension was due partly to the fact that Dad had arrived home late for supper.

Another house rule was Dad's insistence that "supper be on the table at a quarter after five." He got off work at five o'clock. That's when the whistle blew at the plant. It took him fifteen minutes to walk home, and he wanted supper ready when he got there. There was hell to pay if it wasn't. Problem was, he had been coming home late for the past couple of weeks. When Mom asked why he was late, Dad said he had stopped by the bar with his buddies for a beer or two. It was getting to be a problem. Mom didn't like it. I could tell she was mad.

After we finished eating, Mom started to clear the dishes off the table. She picked up the empty bowl of mac 'n' cheese and put the bowl of sliced beets on top. On her way to the kitchen she set down the bowls, picked up a slice of beet, and put it on Dad's left eye.

He sat there for a moment, shocked and stunned. He looked like one of those dogs that have one black eye—only his was purple. Mom was laughing hysterically at how ridiculous he looked. My brother and I joined in the laughter. It was funny—for about three seconds. Dad wasn't laughing. He pushed back from the table, grabbed the bowl of beets, dumped the whole thing on Mom's head, then rubbed them around over her face and in her hair.

I'm sure that words were spoken. I don't remember what they were. Nor do I remember how the scene ended. My brother and I ran outside to play.

Chapter 6:

Beach Days

Abigail was the eldest of Mom's sisters; we called her Aunt Abby. She and Mom hung around together. She and her husband, Ralph, would drive their Buick the five miles south from Beverly to Delanco and pick us up. We'd pile into the car and head for the Jersey Shore.

On good days, it took an hour and a half to drive across the state. On weekends, when the traffic was bad, it might take twice as long. The car was crowded with eight passengers. Uncle Ralph would drive. Aunt Abby rode in the passenger's side with Cousin Freddy on her lap and Cousin Dick sitting between them. In the back, Mom rode behind Uncle Ralph so she could talk to her sister. Dad sat behind Aunt Abby so he could talk to Uncle Ralph. My brother sat between them.

I used to climb up on the shelf between the backseat and the rear window. It was just right for me. It offered a chance to stretch out my legs. The purr of the engine and the noise from the tires on the road would soothe me to sleep. Most of the time I would sleep the whole trip, waking up only when I heard the clickety-clack of the wheels rolling over the cracks between the boards on the causeway between the mainland and Long Beach Island, or the smell of salt in the air as we got closer to the ocean.

When we arrived at the shore, we'd put down a couple of beach blankets, set up the umbrellas, and have a picnic in the shade. Afterwards, we'd play in the sand with our buckets and shovels and splash around in the shallow water. By the end of the day, when it was time to head for home, we were all lobster-red as a result of all that exposure to the sun. Dad said the sun was a good source of vitamin D. (This was decades before anyone knew about SPF.)

By the time we reached home, we were even redder and very sore. The first step of the cure was to sit in a bathtub full of cold water. Dad said that would take away some of the pain. After stepping out of the tub, we dried off and took the second step. That meant Dad would slather Noxzema all over our bodies to treat for burns. This application made us cold all over. We stood there in the bathroom, shivering, until we could climb into our jammies and jump into bed. We couldn't sleep for quite a while, but eventually fatigue took over and, mercifully, we fell asleep.

A few days later, the blisters would show up. After the blisters burst and the fluid came out, the skin started to peel. We couldn't resist pulling off the loose pieces of skin with our fingers. We were pretty miserable for a few days. Nevertheless, we returned to the shore as often as we could each summer.

Chapter 7:

Family Dinners

Most of the fights took place around the evening meal. The supper table became the battleground. The issue was always about Dad coming home late to supper. That's what they fought about. Yet part of me sensed that there was something else going on underneath that I didn't have any words for.

One night, Dad was really late for supper and Mom wasn't happy. She was in a no-win situation. If supper wasn't ready when Dad got home, there would be trouble. Tonight supper was ready, on time, and Dad wasn't home. Mom was mad because she had "slaved over a hot stove" to cook supper. She had busted her butt to have it ready on time. Now it was a quarter to six and Dad was still not home. Mom was keeping supper warm, but there was a chance that it might burn if Dad didn't show up soon.

I sensed how angry and upset Mom was by the set of her face. All the muscles looked tense and she kept wringing her hands.

Six o'clock came and went; still no Dad.

Mom got up from the table. "I'm sick and tired of your father being late," she said. Then she stamped her feet as she walked to the front door.

I heard the deadbolt click as she locked it. *Uh-oh*, I thought. *There's gonna be trouble.*

Mom stomped through the house and I heard the same click as she locked the back door. When she returned to the table she was holding her handkerchief to her nose. She was clearly upset. I felt the tension mounting, a combination of anxiety, fear, and hunger. We had not had supper because one of the rules was, "We can't eat until Dad comes home." He would be furious if we dared to take a bite without him.

"Mommy, can't we eat?" I asked.

"No, not until your father comes home."

"But I'm hungry."

"You'll have to wait."

We were startled by a knocking at the front door. It was loud. It was Dad.

"Open up, Reeb, I can't get in."

The knocking turned to pounding. *Bang, bang, bang.* "Open this door."

Mom started to tremble. I could see her body shaking. She didn't get up.

More pounding, this time at the back door. I heard my dad mumbling something as he returned to the front door but I couldn't make out what he was saying. I heard more loud thumps at the front door, followed by, "Reeb, you open this goddamn door or I'll kick it down!"

Still she sat. We heard a loud crash, made by a combination of wood splintering and glass shattering. My brother and I dove under the table for safety. What happened next I cannot tell—not because it was so awful but because I can't remember. I don't remember having supper that night. I don't remember how the door got fixed. Little Bobby went away that day. He found a place of safety somewhere else.

Chapter 8:

Loss and Change

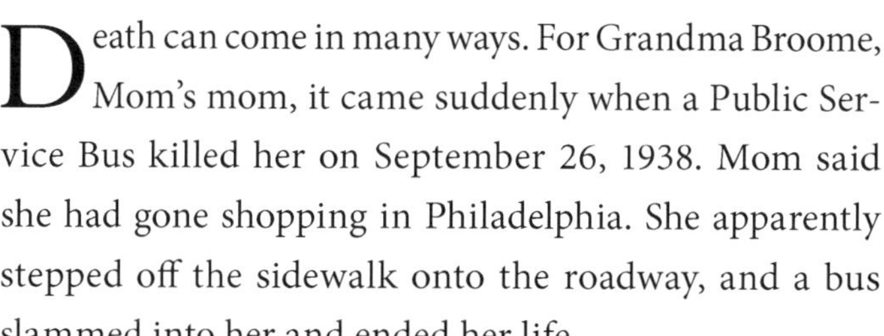

Death can come in many ways. For Grandma Broome, Mom's mom, it came suddenly when a Public Service Bus killed her on September 26, 1938. Mom said she had gone shopping in Philadelphia. She apparently stepped off the sidewalk onto the roadway, and a bus slammed into her and ended her life.

This was another of those events nobody in my family talked about, so I don't have any further details of the accident. I have often wondered: Was she distracted? Was it during rush hour, when everybody's in a hurry to get home? Did someone bump into her and cause her to lose her balance? I have lots of questions, and no answers. I think now that if the bus driver had been at fault there would have been some kind of settlement. But there were no changes in our lifestyle to indicate we ever received such a windfall.

Mary Prudence Brown Broome is a shadow person to me. I don't remember her face or the sound of her voice. As far as I know, no pictures survive. One image of her persists in my memory. I see her seated in the kitchen with a colander on her lap, preparing supper. The sun streaming in through the lace drapes illuminates her left side. One by one she picks a green string bean out of a paper bag, breaks off the stem, discards it, and then snaps the bean in half and drops the pieces into the colander.

Sometimes I'd like to know more, like a photographer in the darkroom waiting for his film to develop, but no matter how hard I try to remember, nothing appears.

After Grandma died, we moved. I'm not sure if we had to move, or if we wanted to. Maybe Mom didn't want to live there anymore—too many memories for her to continue living in that space after her mother died. We moved three houses up the street, to the corner of Hickory and Walnut Streets.

Dad's buddies from work, Otis Walker and Lou Epley, helped us get the new house ready. Mom didn't like the old wallpaper. Too dingy, she said, it would have to go. They removed it by spraying the wall down with water and allowing it to soak for a few minutes before peeling it off with large putty knives. It was a royal mess, Mom said, but it had to be done.

I loved messes and playing with water, so the men assigned me the job of refilling the spray tank, pumping up the pressure, and spraying the walls. After wiping down the walls with vinegar water and allowing them to dry overnight, they sandpapered them smooth and replaced the wallpaper with fresh paint that Mom had picked out. They tore up the tattered carpet and the padding from the floor and took it to the town dump. Next they sanded the hardwood floors to remove the accumulated grime and allow the grain of the wood to show, and applied two coats of varnish. When they were done, the floors glistened. The reflection of light from the windows brightened up the room.

Later, when the paint had dried, Dad rented a truck and Otis and Lou helped us move the heavy furniture into our new home. I helped too. I pulled my red wagon, filled with bags and boxes of my things, along the sidewalk from the old house to the new one. I made sure to bring along Teddy Bear and Bunny, my favorite stuffed animals.

Our new home had a hedge around the front yard. A wooden fence enclosed the back. A covered porch wrapped around the front and left side of the house. It provided protection from the elements, a place to take off your galoshes in the winter and to shake out your bumbershoot after a summer shower. The garage out back was an upgrade from the house at 629.

During this period I struck up a friendship with Ernie Verner, one of my classmates. He lived two blocks away, over on Union Avenue. We both had small bikes with sixteen-inch wheels. We rode all over town together, checking things out. It was mean of me, and unbrotherly, but I loved it when Ernie and I could ride off together on our bikes and leave my little brother in the dust. It was a drag when he was along, limiting our range because he didn't have a bike. Sadly, I wasn't any more patient with him than Dad was with me, a defect of character I worked hard to modify with my own children.

Ernie and I would often race each other on our bikes from St. Miguel Avenue to the Pennsylvania Railroad tracks, a distance of five blocks. It was enough distance to test our staying power. Some days he won. I won the others.

Sometimes we'd ride the other direction, west toward the Delaware River. At the end of the road wooden pilings stood, gray with age, the ghostlike remains of a ferryboat landing. During the 1920s, commuters from New Jersey had taken the ferry downriver to Camden or across the river to north Philadelphia. That was before the Tacony–Palmyra Bridge was built in 1929. The Fathers of Delanco Township had hired trucks to dump a huge pile of topsoil at the end of the road so nobody would drive into the river by accident.

Ernie and I pedaled our bikes at top speed up over

that pile of dirt to see how far we could leap through the air toward the water. The landing took its toll on our bikes, sometimes flattening the wheel and at others bending the fork. It also took its toll on our bodies, inflicting various cuts and abrasions. Somehow, we survived.

Fish loved to spawn and raise their families among these wooden pilings. The water was quiet and out of the main current. Retired guys liked to come there with their fishing poles and bait boxes, hoping for sunfish, bluegills, or perch. One old guy we knew only as Bill used to wet a hook there every day the weather permitted. It was a way to get out of the house and to find some peace and quiet. Young boys don't know much about that.

Most days, Bill was remarkably tolerant of our noise, our incessant stream of questions, and our skipping rocks on the water. But even Bill had a limit to his patience. One day we were sitting there with Bill, watching him fish and disturbing his peace. We were curious about a couple of mayflies that were darting around, hooked together like a jet plane being refueled in the air. Later we learned that they were mating, a foggy concept that I connected to dogs humping on the playground.

I asked Bill what they were doing. He cleared his throat to gain a little time, then dodged the question and cautioned us not to get too close to them—those mayflies, he said, were nicknamed "stitching bugs." If you weren't careful, they'd land on your mouth and sew your lips shut.

That graphic image struck terror into our young

hearts and put an abrupt ending to our visit with Bill. We hopped on our bikes and rode fast to put some distance between us and those stitching bugs. In the classroom a teacher might have said, "Shh, no more talking"; Dad would have said, "You ask too many questions." Bill's solution showed a lot more creative brilliance, and the results were stunningly effective.

On Saturday mornings I loved to go over to Ernie's house to build things with our Erector Sets. After we had built everything pictured in the instructions, we combined our two sets of pieces and made things out of our own creative imaginings.

Mrs. Verner knew how hard we worked on these projects. She understood how important they were to us. They were to be admired and bragged about and exalted over. So we left them there. That was one of the things I loved about Mrs. Verner: she got it. She knew how much it meant to me to come back the following Saturday and find our project still there. It didn't go away. It would take years before I realized how incredibly sensitive that was of her, to understand that I was still smarting over the loss of my mom.

Santa brought us a new sled for Christmas 1938, a Flexible Flyer. Most of the kids in the neighborhood got sleds for a single rider, but ours was long enough for two. Dad tied a rope to the front so he could pull us through the snow when we went shopping at Voight's corner store. There was room for my brother and me plus a couple of bags of groceries.

We were heartbroken when somebody stole that sled from our front porch in January. We had only had it a couple of weeks and suddenly it was gone.

Here's how we got it back: We slept in the front bedroom on the second floor of our new house, overlooking the intersection of Hickory and Walnut Streets. A streetlight illuminated this crossroad from the northeast side. One of the house rules was that we had to come home when the streetlights came on. One night I heard a commotion outside, down on the street, so I pulled the curtains aside to get a better view. I could see a bunch of older boys gathered under the streetlight. They had to be older because they were still outside after dark. They were waiting there for cars to slow down at the intersection so they could grab hold of the bumper and "hitch a ride." During the lull between rides they stood around, smoked, told jokes, and huddled together to try to stay warm. I could see their breath as they spoke. They held their sleds upright with the back of the runners stuck in the snow so they'd be ready when a car came by.

I noticed that one of the sleds was taller than the rest. Instantly, I knew in my gut that it was our sled. I called Dad upstairs to our bedroom so he could have a look.

"That's our sled," I told him.

At first he was skeptical.

"See, Dad?" I persisted. "It has three braces on the runners. Nobody else in the neighborhood has a sled with three braces. All their sleds have two. That's our sled."

To his credit, he believed me. He went downstairs, put on his coat and hat, and walked across the street to confront them. Ken and I could see them talking. After a couple of exchanges, the boy with our sled picked it up, handed it to Dad, and ran off into the night.

In a home where adults didn't talk about things and children were supposed to be seen and not heard, where affirmation and support were rare, Dad had listened. I could hardly believe it.

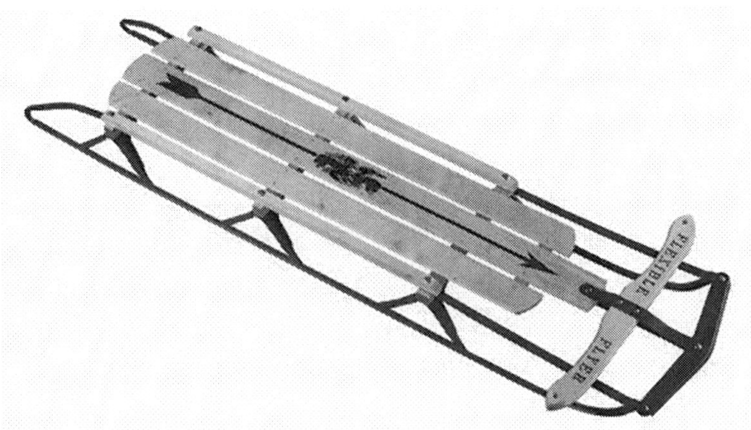

Flexible Flyer Steel Runner Sled

Chapter 9:

Good Times

One Saturday morning when I was eight I got up early to mow the grass while it was still cool. I had finished my mowing and now was busy clipping the hedge that surrounded our yard on two sides.

Mom and Dad came out on the front porch together. Dad asked if I wanted to go to Riverside with him to the Firestone hardware store. I told him I wanted to finish trimming the hedge before it got too hot.

"I think you'd better go with your father," Mom chimed in.

That seemed strange, but something in her voice was convincing. So I put my hedge clippers on the porch and joined my dad.

We walked together, hand in hand. It was only a mile to the neighboring town. We had to cross the Rancocas Creek on our way, so I picked up a few stones to throw into the water as we crossed the bridge.

When we walked into the store I noticed a banner that said, "Bicycle Sale." Dad started looking at bicycles. One stood out above all the rest. It was a Roadmaster with chrome handlebars and chrome fenders. It was forest green and had a chain guard, a battery-operated horn, and a toolkit fitted between the crossbar. We called the crossbar the "ball-buster," because that's what happened if the chain broke while you were standing up and pedaling hard.

Dad asked me if I liked the bike.

"I love it," I said. "Why?"

"It's yours if you want it," he said.

My mind was in a tizzy. This was an amazing stroke of good fortune, the best thing I could remember ever having happened in my life. It was hard to take it in. *This bike for me?* I thought. A part of me thought I must be dreaming. Yet Dad was already at the cash register, making arrangements to pay for the bike in installments. This beauty was mine. All mine.

We had to walk the bike home. We didn't have a car, and I didn't know how to ride a "big-wheeler" yet. I had ridden an eighteen-inch bike for some time, but a step up to a twenty-six-incher was huge. It would take some practice before I could do that. And my new bike was way too wonderful to risk a crash.

The forest-green Roadmaster

When we got home, Dad took me to the school playground across the street so I could practice riding the bigger bike. He ran alongside me as I pedaled, holding on to the back of the seat to keep me from falling. We tried it a few times, then Dad said he needed to rest for a spell. He lit a cigarette, and after he caught his breath we tried again. This time I got the feel of it and rode away on my own. I felt flooded with a variety of feelings—of freedom, of pride in my shiny new bike, and of accomplishment for having learned to ride it.

A couple of times each summer Dad's work buddies, Walker and Epley, would invite him (and me, by extension) to go fishing "down Tucker-ging." The real name of the town was Tuckerton, but for them it was always "Tucker-ging."

I loved this for two reasons: first, it was a great adventure; second, I got to go along and my brother didn't. Later, I would learn about sibling rivalry. For now, it just felt like payback for some of the hours I'd lost with Dad while Mom was in the hospital having my brother and afterward, as she recovered from the damage to her birth canal. I was mad about the separation, so these trips to the shore helped make up for some of that lost time—to balance the scales that had been thrown out of whack by the events surrounding my brother's birth.

The drive took between an hour and an hour and a half. About halfway we would stop at Ott's Elbow Room. It provided a timely spot to stretch our legs, use the restroom, and grab a bite to eat. The men would order a ham and cheese on rye and a beer; I'd have a BLT with chips and a birch beer. I felt like such a big shot, sitting on a bar stool flanked by Dad and his buddies. Dad said the food was cheaper at a bar because they made their money on the booze.

Refreshed by this stop, we'd pile in the car and complete the second half of the trip. In no time we'd arrive in Tuckerton, a small resort town and fishing village on Barnegat Bay, north of Atlantic City. We'd rent a motorboat and fish for flounder. There was beer in the cooler on the boat, but I don't recall anybody getting out of control.

When I was seven I was in Mrs. Williams' third-grade class at Hickory Street Elementary School. Each morning before school two smells crept up the stairs and made their way into our bedroom: one aromatic, from the coffee perking on the gas stove; the other the acrid smell of tobacco from the Lucky Strike that hung loosely from Dad's lower lip.

These smells were welcome and familiar. I got out of bed, pushed my feet into my slippers, and quietly made my way downstairs so as not to wake my brother. Dad was having breakfast. Every morning he had a smoke, a cup of coffee, and two slices of Wonder Bread toasted and slathered with butter. I loved mornings. Mornings were my time with Dad. Breakfast was a time of olfactory delights: coffee, cigarette smoke, Old Spice aftershave, and Vitalis on his hair—smells of Dad. He grabbed me under the arms, gave me a hug, then planted me on his knee. He dipped his toast in the coffee, took a bite, dipped it again, and offered me a bite. We traded bites until it was gone. Then it was time to leave for work. He'd hug me again and kiss me good-bye. I'd wave as he went down the front steps.

Dad walked to work and back home again each day, about a mile each way. We didn't have a car. Getting to class was not a problem; we lived right across the street from the school.

I must have been curious about why we didn't own a car, because one day Dad took out a piece of paper so he could show me how the accident happened. He drew an intersection on the paper with an arrow coming up from the bottom of the page: "I was coming this way." He drew a second arrow coming from the right side of the page: "He was coming this way. When we saw each other, both of us swerved sharply to avoid an accident. The cars didn't hit each other, but the change in direction threw the other driver's wife against the passenger door. The door flew open and she was hurled from the car. Her forward progress was stopped as she struck a fire hydrant. The impact caused substantial facial injuries. The woman was hospitalized for some time and needed surgical reconstruction of her face. The medical bills were substantial, so the woman sued for damages. When the case was heard, the judge found both drivers equally at fault."

Dad paused for a moment before he continued. His face tightened up and some bitterness about the injustice of the whole incident crept into his voice as he said, "She sued us both, but she never collected from her husband."

My guess is that Dad couldn't afford to make medical payments to the woman and payments for the automobile at the same time. That's why we didn't own a car.

Chapter 10:

Life After

Shortly after Mom died, I turned nine. If there was a party, it couldn't have been much. Too much sadness in the air. And while nothing of that birthday would stay with me, what did etch itself on my heart and in my mind is something that would happen forty-five years later, while I was unpacking cartons after a move. I came across a familiar object: a red hardcover book about an inch and a half thick with the title *Modern Postage Stamp Album* on the front cover with an airplane flying over the New York City skyline.

I gasped at finding this musty old friend, which had once ranked up top with Teddy Bear on my list of treasured possessions. I opened the cover to look inside. My heart jumped up in my throat as I read the inscription:

"Bobby Finertie, October 2, 1941," written in the flowing hand of Aunt Abby, Mom's older sister. My eyes burned hot with tears that overflowed and made their way down my cheeks. This was a gift she'd presented to me less than a month after Mom died. As a kid, I hadn't understood that this stamp album was as an act of love and grace by an aunt who was herself full of grief at the loss of her sister. Now I understood that she'd wanted to help little Bobby take his mind off the loss of his mom, to bring some joy into a life overwhelmed by sadness.

Mom was the one who always took the family pictures, with her Kodak Brownie box camera. After she died, the pictures stopped. My nurturing stopped, too. Her camera was blue. I was too.

Ken and I stayed with Nana and Grandpa on Carroll Street in Riverside for a while until Dad could find someone to care for us. That's when the migraine headaches began.

The nation was still in the throes of the Great Depression at that point. Dad had a decent job. Many did not. There was not a lot of money there to pay for childcare.

When the dust settled around this issue, our caregiver was Aunt Belle Maloy. Technically she was not our aunt, but that's what we called her. It was the shorthand we invented for Mom's younger sister Jessie's mother-in-law.

To describe Aunt Belle as a large woman would be

a kindness. Seeing her pause at a doorway and then turn sideways so she could get through would help you get your mind around her fullness. We would have called her fat, but that word was not permitted in our family. The approved word was "full-bodied."

I think Aunt Belle undertook the job as caregiver because she was the only one available—or, perhaps, the only one available at the price offered, which couldn't have been much. I believe that she meant well and gave it her best shot. It could not have been easy, given that both Ken and I resented her (unfairly) simply because she wasn't our mom. We missed Mom savagely and were not willing to accept love and care from anyone else who was not her.

Aunt Belle had little control over us. We reminded her often that she was not our mom and therefore not the boss of us. Even if she had a mind to exert some discipline—and she often did—her great size prevented her from ever catching us. Looked at one way, we were thankless little imps. But the reality is, we were deeply wounded little boys who were crushed by grief over the sudden and unexpected loss of our mom—two little guys doing their level best to try to keep their heads above water in a tempestuous sea of sorrow. And the don't-talk rule of our family system prevented any discussion of the loss that might have helped us to process the grief and lessen our sorrow.

Since Aunt Belle was unable to catch us in order to impose any discipline, the system devolved to keeping a record of the various infractions we committed while Dad was at work so he could decide what punishments he thought we deserved when he got home. When Mom was alive, we used to love to wait on the front porch for Dad to come home from work. When we saw him coming, we would run to greet him, and then the three of us would walk together back to the house.

The joy of this happy reunion with our dad after a day of separation eroded over time, however, and during our time with Aunt Belle, it morphed into a time of fear and dread. It was a time of reverse alchemy, a time when gold turned into lead. We knew we had several infractions on the ledger every day and we knew what that meant: the belt. It seemed to us that try as we might, we were unable to live a blemish-free life. We tried to be perfect, not realizing that our goal was a *Mission: Impossible.* We fell short every day. Small wonder, then, that I should later embark on a spiritual quest to find a loving Father in heaven—someone who could love me with my faults and forgive my shortcomings in a way my earthly father didn't seem to understand.

After Mom died on Labor Day of 1941, our time at 635 Hickory Street became a period when home was not to be found. "Be a good boy" became my mantra during this time. It rang in my ears like tinnitus. It stuck in my brain like a haunting refrain.

I did my little-boy best to obey Mom's deathbed directive. I think she meant it as a blessing. It was her way of trying to guide me after she knew she wasn't going to be there to do it herself. At best, however, it was a mixed blessing. Because it was her last request, I put a halo on it, ramped up the expectations, and found myself unable to live up to those heavenly standards.

One of the ways I did feel I could follow Mom's directive was to get good grades in school. So I did. I had been blessed at birth with a bright mind that made school seem easy. In addition, nothing pleased me more than seeing a gold star at the top of my class papers when the teacher returned our assignments.

I was in the third grade when Mom died. Mrs. Williams was my teacher. She became my very first surrogate mom. Her name headed a long list of woman teachers I would fall in love with and do my best to please over the years. This marked the onset of an unconscious strategy to please others in my search for love.

None of those gold-star papers survived, but it would be difficult to overestimate how important they were to me. Didn't they offer incontestable proof that I was being a good boy? Wouldn't Mom be pleased?

Chapter 11:

Filling the Void

Because of the lack of nurturing at home, I sought the love I needed at my friends' homes. Their moms became surrogate moms to me. One of these was the Tevises', where I played Monopoly with Dick and Ken most Saturday mornings. I also loved going there because Mrs. Tevis made us grilled cheese sandwiches served up with thin slices of tomato and chocolate milk from Bishop's Dairy, located only a few doors away next to the firehouse. Her acts of caring felt like love to me—like an April shower watering the thirsty places of my heart.

On Saturday evenings I learned to play double-deck pinochle at Leonard Smith's house. Mrs. Smith entertained the neighborhood with card games and snacks. Her homemade popcorn was the best, and it was something we couldn't afford when we went to the movies. As soon as the bowl started running low she'd head for the kitchen to pop some more. It was her way of keeping us off the streets and out of trouble. I soaked in her TLC like a dry sponge.

When school was closed for holidays, I'd go out into the country to the farm where Warren Russ lived. His mom was a schoolteacher, so she had lots of fun things for us to do. I loved playing Chinese checkers and Hangman, and putting together jigsaw puzzles.

All of these women were mother-surrogates for me. I think they liked me. People warmed up to me quickly. I don't think they doted on me, or treated me any differently than they did their own children. I felt they enjoyed being moms. They weren't preoccupied with something else they'd rather be doing or daydreaming about someplace they'd rather be. They liked the nurturing role, and I liked being in their presence. They were mindful and available. It made all the difference in the world to me having them there, accented by the contrast of my own mom not being there. I was as comfortable in their presence as a cat curled up on the carpet in front of the fireplace.

Shaking up the serenity of that scene and rumbling like an active volcano alongside it, of course, was the ache I felt for one of Mom's hugs, for the love in her eyes as she looked at me or wetted her fingers with her tongue to try to tame my resistant cowlick, and the gnawing emptiness of life without her.

Chapter 12:

Stepmother

I was eleven when dad married Julia Taylor on April 7, 1944. She was the receptionist at Zurbrugg Memorial Hospital. Initially she put her best foot forward and tried to win us over. Calling her "Mom" was out of the question, so we agreed to call her Jule.

Before many months had passed, Jule had become the stepmother of fiction, the mother we didn't want. Ken and I resented her from the start. Both of us wanted our real mom back, not this stranger we didn't know and didn't like. I kept aloof from Jule, saving a special place in my heart for Mom to come back. I had zero understanding of why Mom had gone away or where she had gone. I didn't know when she would be coming back home, but I still thought there was a chance she might.

Our time with Aunt Belle, although difficult, was temporary. Ken and I knew that. So we sucked it up and did the best we could, hoping that at some point Mom would come back and our family life would return to normal.

After Dad married Jule, those hopes were dashed. Our new normal slammed me right in the gut. Jule was not at all the person I wanted or imagined as caregiver, yet her marriage to Dad made it permanent. Like it or not, this was how our new life was going to be.

In fairness to all, I think each of us was trying our best to do a difficult thing that none of us had any practice at or knew how to do. Dad was brand-new at being Jule's husband. Jule, meanwhile, had just switched roles from hospital employee to wife, homemaker, and stepmother. Ken and I were grieving the loss of our real mom and tying to wrap our minds around the notion of loving a stepmother we scarcely knew. It was a scenario designed to deliver a lot of disappointed expectations and distance.

Jule had strong ideas about how kids should comport themselves, her own childlessness notwithstanding. She was bound and determined to shape us up into her vision of how young boys should be and behave. I defied her every step of her stepmother way. It seemed to me that she didn't know or care about what I wanted. At school I was compliant, got good grades, and often received gold stars on my papers. I was not disruptive in class and did my best to please the teacher. At home, in contrast, Jule found only defects in my character, pointed them out to Dad at every opportunity, and stood by with a smirk on her face while I was being punished. Before long, home became a place I dreaded to return to after school.

Tears well up and burn my eyes as I write this. I wonder if this was when I began to hate myself.

Dad got me a bow and arrow for my twelfth birthday. My favorite pastime was to gather up this bow and the quiver of arrows and take them to the field across the street. What a sweet diversion to shoot the arrows into the air, watch where they landed, and retrieve them so I could do it again. I spent hours amusing myself in that way, pretending I was Tonto, the Lone Ranger's trusty sidekick.

At some point, Jule became afraid that some other child in the neighborhood might be injured during this activity. This never was an actual problem because most of the time I was out there by myself, having a good time. Second, at the times when other kids were present, they stood with me as I shot the arrows, helped me keep track of where they landed, and then helped me go retrieve them so we could shoot them again. It was a harmless activity; just a bunch of kids having a good time on the playground. No one was ever hurt during the process.

Nevertheless, Jule's obsessive, irrational fear prevailed. My bow was confiscated and hidden away where I couldn't find it. The only explanation I ever received was, "Somebody's liable to be hurt." Indeed somebody was hurt—me. I felt a profound sense of loss of my favorite toy and a feeling of deprivation of my joy. I sensed in Jule a smug satisfaction that she'd gotten her way at my expense. I had no evidence that any adult considered supervising the activity so no one would be injured; there was only a search and seizure. This irrational, punitive action did much to kindle the fires of resentment between Jule and me.

This was not the only clash between us. Around this time, I fell in love with hamsters. I saw some in the window one day as Dad and I went to the Firestone hardware store. I liked the softness of their fur; the cute way they stuffed sunflower seeds in the pouches inside their cheeks; the way they ran around the wire wheel to get their exercise and climbed through the plastic tunnels.

I pestered Dad until he agreed to buy a pair. We got a wire cage, some cedar chips for the bottom (I love that smell), and some mixed seeds for food. We set them up a house on top of a chest of drawers under the stairs that led down to the cellar.

This was a compromise location. My brother and I wanted them in our bedroom, but Jule forbade them any space in the part of the house where we lived. "They remind me too much of a rat," she said.

We were excited to have these pets. We spent time with them before breakfast and after school. We checked to make sure they had food and water every day. Once a week we'd put them in our pocket while we put fresh wood chips on the bottom of the cage. We watched them with joy as they frolicked, chased each other around, and played piggy-back.

As the weeks passed by the female grew bigger, until Dad finally declared that she must be pregnant. We could hardly contain our excitement. We had never seen anything being born. Jule expressed her displeasure at having more rats running around the basement.

I sensed that the female's secretiveness might mean she was getting ready to have her babies. I made frequent checks, but her reclusiveness meant I couldn't see what was happening. On Monday morning, I hurried down the stairs to look in on the momma-to-be. To my great surprise and astonishment, I saw her in plain view with a tangle of baby hamsters wriggling around like a ball of fishing worms.

What I'd read about hamsters indicated that the pups needed relatively low light while they were young, and that quiet was essential. Loud noises might cause the momma to fear for the safety of her pups and, in an instinctive maternal move, stuff them into her cheek pouches to keep them safe. If they were in there too long, they could suffocate and die.

During that era, Monday was the day everybody washed clothes and hung them outside to dry, so I knew Jule would be up and down the stairs doing the laundry. I asked her to please be as quiet as possible as she went up and down the stairs. I was not reassured when she said, "You'd better get yourself off to school before you're late, young man, I'll take care of the laundry."

Throughout that day I thought about the hamsters and wondered how they were doing. When the last bell rang at school, I ran home to check on the babies. The mamma was there in the middle of the cage. In front of her was a lifeless mass of gray fur. My worst fears had come true.

I burst into tears. I couldn't stop crying. I felt inconsolable. I had been so excited about the new life. Now there was more death. Eight baby hamsters had died, and in my mind I could picture Jule stomping up and down the stairs as loudly as she could, trying to make sure none of those baby rats survived.

It was about more than just the hamsters, clearly. I was grieving for those little ones, no doubt, but some of my tears were the ones I hadn't been able to shed when Mom died.

These incidents with the bow and arrow and the hamsters stoked the fires of my anger and kept my stomach tied in knots. They also widened the chasm between Jule and me. There was none of the warmth and closeness I was so hungry for. But the crowning act of brutality, the last straw, was when Jule drove away my aunts and forbade them to come to the house. By cutting me off from Mom's sisters, she deprived me of the best hope I had for nurturing.

At the time I was only vaguely aware that I never got to see my aunts anymore, but many years later, while I was visiting Aunt Jessie in Florida, she'd tell me, "We always loved you, Bobby, but Jule told us not to come to the house anymore." That act of unkindness was the most difficult to forgive. I would wrestle for years to let go of my anger and bitterness around that.

My holding on to that resentment never hurt Jule a bit, of course; instead, it festered inside me and made me miserable. When I came to the place where I had suffered enough, I finally forgave her and set myself free. A good friend's comment captured what this experience was for me when he said, "Bob, some of us get it right away, while others get it more deeply."

Chapter 13:

Coping Mechanisms

In October 1945, Dad surprised me with a BB gun for my thirteenth birthday. And this wasn't just any old BB gun, it was a Daisy Red Rider with a lever action, just like in the movies, with a piece of rawhide tied around the saddle ring so it wouldn't fall out of the scabbard as the cowboys rode fast chasing the Indians. I had seen a picture of one in the Sears catalog and pestered him for some time to get one for me.

These kinds of things required a delicate negotiation. If I pressed too hard or too often, Dad would unbuckle his belt. But I noticed that after Mom died, he softened a bit and caved in to my requests at times, as though he were trying to make up for the loss we all felt. Even following the Great Depression years, and with World War II raging, shopping was a mood elevator. Nothing beat the sight and smell and feel of something new, even when we knew down deep that the pleasure would be fleeting.

The backyard of our new house offered an ideal place to learn to shoot my BB gun. The garage provided a backstop to prevent BBs from straying into the neighbor's yard. I drew bull's-eyes on the ends of empty cardboard boxes and aimed at them. I felt great satisfaction punching holes in those targets and learning to tighten my groups. For variety I'd place empty soup cans and mayonnaise bottles on top of the boxes and shoot at them. I enjoyed the ping as the BBs tore through the tin cans. I relished the sound of breaking glass when I shot the bottles. This harmless destruction helped give a voice to all the anger I felt about Mom going away. I was mad as a hornet about feeling abandoned; shooting was an outlet for some of that rage.

Most of the time I shot lead BBs because they were cheap and plentiful, even during the war. During one of my trips to the local hardware store, however, the owner talked me into trying some new copper-clad BBs. I bought a hundred to try them out. They came in a cardboard cylinder about the size of a roll of pennies. Lead BBs worked fine on most of my targets—they could penetrate cardboard, tin cans, and glass jars—but they bounced off of milk bottles, which were made of thicker glass. I was anxious to see if the copper-clads could break them.

I poured a handful of those gleaming beauties into the cylinder of my Red Rider and drew down on the target. I squeezed the trigger and let out a yelp of joy as I saw a puff of white smoke at the point of impact and watched the milk bottle I'd just shot shatter into a pile of pieces. After that demonstration I always got copper-clads, even though it meant I would have fewer shots since they were more expensive.

Over time I refined my shooting skills and became quite a good shot with that Daisy, able to hit clothespins on the head, Popsicle sticks, and pennies at will. One day while I was shooting, a chipping sparrow landed in our tree and broke forth in song. What happened next was inevitable. After I saw him fall off the limb and heard him hit the ground, I was overcome with a huge wave of remorse. I knew I shouldn't have done it. How would I explain this? How could I avoid a thrashing?

I considered what it would be like, though, if I were a hunter. I decided to get my game, cook it, and eat it. I figured that if I hadn't shot it just for fun, if I hadn't enjoyed murdering that sparrow but had shot it for food, all would be okay. So I built a little campfire using my Boy Scout skills. Then I plucked the feathers off the bird, skewered him on a stick, and had roast sparrow for supper.

I sure felt strange eating such a tiny drumstick. It tasted like chicken, all right, but it would have taken a bunch of them to make a meal—probably about the same amount as nightingale tongues.

One day Dad asked me to fix the fence in the backyard. Some of the boards had come loose at the bottom and allowed our mutt, Schming, to prowl the neighborhood. No garbage can was safe from his raids. The neighbors were furious about his forays and not shy about informing us of their displeasure and their opinion about the doubtful moral character of his ancestors.

I got a hammer and nails from the garage and set to work mending the fence. As I hit the nails with the hammer I heard a musical tone, not unlike the one sounded by the triangle I played in the first grade rhythm band. The nail produced one tone going through the board, a second tone as the nail penetrated the two-by-four bracing, and a third as I drove it into the top of the post. These notes were harmonic and hypnotizing.

Before long, the repairs were over and the concert began. I was a world-renowned conductor orchestrating all the tones into a symphony. Lost in that fantasy, I kept pounding away until the nails were gone. This musical interlude not only soothed the angry child within but also served as a harmless way to vent some of my anger about Mom's death.

Dad took a different view. Didn't I know there was a war going on? That steel was expensive? That nails were scarce? I had been wasteful. He unbuckled his belt.

Chapter 14:

Counting the Minutes

Most of what happened at high school felt awkward, painful, or forgettable. I went out for football to impress the girls and got a broken tibia in my left leg to show for it. The girls were not impressed, but some of them did come to visit me at home and sign my cast.

My dad and Jule were obsessed with having me socialized. They dragged me off on Wednesday evenings with my heels dug in to the Community Center so I could talk and dance and mix with other kids. I hated it. I didn't know how to dance and had no interest in learning. I played Ping-Pong most of the time instead and found that enjoyable. I avoided the bathroom for as long as I could because a couple of the town bullies hung out there and messed with me when I went in there.

One of the ways I coped during these troubled years was by listening to music. This was the 1950s, and television was in its infancy. There were very few programs. A lot of channels showed test patterns most of the time. Radio was hot. The airwaves were full of songs by Frank Sinatra, Perry Como, Patti Page, Eddie Fisher, and Mario Lanza. One of my favorites was Barry Manilow. The lyrics of his songs helped me identify what was going on in me, and how I was feeling. I learned the words to "All the Time" by heart. Manilow sang of his own struggles growing up feeling alone, different, left out, and not belonging. It helped me to know that I wasn't the only one feeling that way.

One of the highlights of high school was starring in the junior play. I loved acting and being in the spotlight. Looking at one of the publicity pictures of this event many years later, I'd cringe at seeing how uncomfortable I felt in close quarters with my leading lady. She adored me—and scared the bejeebers out of me.

Another memorable moment happened during my senior year. A barbershop quartet I sang in at a full school assembly got a standing ovation for our rendition of "That Lucky Old Sun." Some people would say, "You done good." Well, good enough for the school principal to grant a five-minute extension of assembly so we could do an encore number. The fear factor ramped up

With Polly Goss, in the junior play

considerably when we got accepted to audition for *Ted Mack's Amateur Hour* later that year.

Puberty for me was an event that amplified my turmoil and confusion. My body was telling me one thing, urgently, and my parents were telling me another—warning of the hazards of STDs and pregnancy. Jule was acting the perfect storm trooper/detective, examining my underwear and bedclothes for evidence of sexual activity so she could make a full report to Dad. I hated her. What she and Dad didn't know and wouldn't understand was that for me this was the time of a perpetual erection—that I couldn't fall asleep until I had some relief from this sexual tension. Of course, they couldn't know and I couldn't tell them. The no-talk rule precluded that.

I wanted to be out of that house at my first opportunity. I thought my chance had arrived when, at high school graduation, the superintendent of schools handed me a full academic scholarship to Juniata College in Pennsylvania along with my diploma. Dad and Jule never said a thing about it. I felt so proud of myself and this accomplishment—but if they shared my feelings, they never said so. On the contrary, the scholarship was never spoken of again. Life returned to normal, which meant the no-talk rule remained in place. We didn't discuss anything except how I'd screwed up this time and what the punishment would be. While other families were excited about having one of their kids going to college and making plans to visit the campus, I took a job as a lifeguard at the local lake that summer.

I think because neither Dad nor Jule had gone to college themselves, it would have been difficult for them to imagine what that was like or what preparations they would need to make to allow it to happen. Besides, times were tough and money was scarce. They were probably looking forward to the time when I would transition from being a dependent to a moneymaker who could contribute to the family income.

Dad was a third-generation Irish immigrant—a blue-collar worker, like his father, with a proud history of employment at the Keystone Watch Case and Riverside Metal Companies. Expecting that I would follow in his footsteps, Dad got me a job in the quality control lab at Riverside Metal Company that fall.

I worked there for three years while living at home. Dad said I had to pay a token rent because I had a job. It wasn't awful. I enjoyed my job. The routine of testing samples of the wire and sheet metal that the company made offered a lot of variety and kept me interested. It was an entry-level job, so the pay was low. But it was enough to pay my room and board and still have some cash left over. I set aside some money from each paycheck and started saving to buy a car.

One of the guys in the neighborhood had a '41 Chevy that he'd souped up with a '46 Chevy engine. He repainted it a deep forest green so it looked like it had just come out of the dealer's showroom. I had the hots for that car. By the end of my first year at work, I had saved enough to buy it. I had the only car in the family.

One winter morning when the temperature had dipped below zero, Dad asked if he could drive my car to run an errand. I said sure. During that trip, the fan belt broke without Dad knowing it. Without the fan to cool the engine, it overheated before he knew what was wrong. He said afterward that he heard something go ping as he was driving but didn't know what it was. It wouldn't have been productive to ask why he didn't pull over to the side of the road to check.

It was only when the car wouldn't go any farther that Dad did pull over to the side of the road. Steam was coming out from under the hood. When he opened it up, smoke billowed out; the engine smelled burnt and made a crackling sound as it cooled. He called a service truck to tow it home. The tow truck man said the engine was all burned up.

I was crushed with disappointment. My "new" car was ruined. Dad never offered to fix it or pay to have it fixed. I felt furious about that. There wasn't any extra money for emergencies like that. There was, however, always money to buy cigarettes and booze. That made me even madder.

I filled my evenings after work pumping iron in an attic gym with Bob Harding, my best childhood friend. This provided an outlet for some of my anger. Afterward, we'd shower and dress and head to the Riverside Roller Rink. Both of us loved to skate dance to the live organ music. The rink closed at eleven, but we'd stay afterward to practice our freestyle routines.

I wanted to get out of the house, to escape the painful dysfunction there, but I didn't know how to do it. I wasn't earning enough to support myself and move out. The fires of rebellion were burning, but always tempered by the "be a good boy" message ringing in my ears.

Three years passed before I got my next chance to get out of there.

Part II

"Whom shall I send, and who will go for us?"

—Isaiah 6:8

Chapter 15:

The Call

I was twenty the summer of 1953. I had now worked in the quality control lab at Riverside Metal Company for three years, and I still found the work challenging and satisfying. The wide variety of tests I performed kept monotony at bay. It wasn't like working on an assembly line. And my boss, Bud Tursi, appreciated me. He encouraged me to enroll in night classes at Drexel Institute of Technology in Philadelphia and promoted me to assistant metallographer.

In this new position, I learned to prepare samples to view on a photomicroscope. For example, the company produced copper sheets from which "slugs" were punched and sent to the United States Mint in Philadelphia, where they were stamped in dies that impressed the image of

Lincoln on the front (head side) and the Lincoln Memorial on the back (tail side).

Riverside Metal Company also manufactured and shipped coils of copper wire to General Electric for use in the windings of their electric motors. The Stewart Warner Company used beryllium copper flat stock made at RMC in the production of their precision gauges. Samples of every lot produced in the foundry were tagged and sent to the lab for testing. After recording them in a daily logbook, I polished them on a buffing wheel, etched them with acid, and viewed them on a photomicroscope. This apparatus magnified the grain size of the sample from one hundred to one thousand times to enable the human eye to see it, and projected the image on a screen. By comparing the on-screen results with reference copies of known grain size, I could make sure that lot met the customer's standards.

Some companies specified only a Rockwell test, which measured the hardness or softness of the metal; others needed their product to fall within certain parameters of tensile strength (how much it could resist being pulled apart) or ductility (how much could it stretch without rupturing). This last quality was important to Frankford Arsenal, where they took the brass stock we sent them and formed it into cartridge cases during World War II. I performed all these tests in the lab.

I was mostly content with my job; it fit with my introverted nature and the obsessive-compulsive part of me that needed order, structure, and sameness. But the bulk of the work involved interacting with *things*—and somewhere deep down, I was gradually becoming aware of a desire to interact more with people, to establish a connection with others. At the same time I was resisting that, afraid to let anybody get close—a self-defeating choice designed to avoid future hurt from abandonment, though I wouldn't know that until later.

Occasionally I had to hand-carry test results to a different department. Sometimes I stopped by to visit someone along the way. Word got back to my boss about it. He called me into his office and said, "We frown upon that, Bob." Being called on the carpet for socializing didn't fit the image of a good boy, so I reformed. But that confrontation helped me to know I didn't want to spend the rest of my life working with things. Whatever work I ended up doing would involve people.

In July of that summer a guest preacher, Bob Lamont, came to fill the pulpit at our Presbyterian church in Delanco while our pastor was away on vacation. He took as his text for the message that day the sixth chapter of Isaiah, the story of Isaiah's call to be a prophet:

> "In the year that King Uzziah died (740 BC) I saw the LORD sitting on a throne, lofty and

> exalted. The seraphim who attended him called out to each other: 'Holy, Holy, Holy is the LORD of Hosts, the whole earth is full of His glory.' The foundations trembled and the temple was filled with smoke."

Think rock concert and special effects. In the presence of the Holy One, Isaiah knew his own shortcomings and said:

> "'Woe is me, for I am ruined. I am a man of unclean lips.' Then one of the seraphim flew to me, with a burning coal in his hand, which he had taken from the altar with tongs. And he touched my mouth with it and said, 'Behold, this has touched your lips; your iniquity is taken away, and your sins are forgiven.'"

What relief I felt hearing that statement. It was a breath of fresh air, a soothing balm. I too had missed the mark a lot and needed forgiveness. At home, messages of shame and punishment dominated the airwaves. There were never any words of forgiveness.

> "Then I heard the voice of the Lord saying, 'Whom shall I send, and who will go for us?'
> I said, Here I am. Send me."

As Bob Lamont spoke these last five words, he looked straight at me. A shudder ran through my body as the truth sank in that he meant this message for me. I knew deep down that this was my call to ministry. I said yes. God had plans for me.

Later that month, when Bill Shea, our pastor, returned from vacation, I shared this moment with him. I didn't know then that my decision would mean four years of college—something no one in our family had ever done—and another three years in seminary after that. It looked like a pretty tall mountain to climb.

"Lord," I prayed, "I don't know how this is going to happen, but I put my life in your hands believing that if this is what you want, you'll provide the way."

He did. Bill Shea was my mentor during this time. All this was terra incognita to me; like the crew of the Enterprise on *Star Trek*, I was venturing where no one in my family had dared to tread.

Bill helped me sort through my choices among schools. The University of Pennsylvania was just across the river in Philadelphia. I could live at home and commute to Penn. I rejected that option out of hand. I did not want to stay at home. Every bone in my body wanted to get out of that house and environment. The second choice was Maryville College in east Tennessee, a Presbyterian liberal arts school founded in 1819 that was well known for its record of preparing people for the ministry. I latched on to Maryville like a free electron to a receptive atom. Casting my lot with the Mighty Scots was my ticket to freedom. I had some fear and trepidation, but not an ounce of hesitation. That decision would prove to be one of the best of my sometimes-impulsive choices.

Bill Shea walked me through the selection process and guided my steps along the path to admission and enrollment. With his help, I prepared to travel to Tennessee and begin my freshman year at Maryville that fall.

Before I left for school, my coworkers at the lab threw me a going-away luncheon and presented me a matched set of luggage for the trip. After packing my bags, I loaded them into my uncle Ed's Chevy and we headed south to Tennessee.

Chapter 16:

Spreading My Wings

In September of 1953, I matriculated as a freshman at Maryville College. One of the elders from our church paid my tuition. I worked on the dish crew at school to pay for meals. I paid for books by applying Dewey Decimal numbers in gold leaf to the spines of books in the college library with a wood-burning tool.

On Saturday mornings, I did yard work for one of the local neighbors to earn some pocket money. I got up early those mornings so I could rake the leaves and mow the lawn in peace. I loved the rustle of new-fallen leaves and the smell of newly mown grass. I felt the chill of the fall air on my hands and face as I raked, even as I broke a sweat from the effort of the raking. It was the time of year when the smell in the air offered a silent reminder that football season and the homecoming parade and dance were just around the corner.

When I had a job to do, my obsessive-compulsive style meant that I would start the job and power on through until I was finished. I often got blisters on my hands from raking. I was hard on myself.

Mrs. Ross, the neighbor, was kinder and more gracious to me than I was to myself. The job normally took me about two and a half hours; halfway through, she would come out into the yard in her apron with a tray of peanut butter cookies fresh out of the oven and a pitcher of lemonade. The aroma of those cookies arrived before she did. "You must be tired," she'd say, "don't you want to take a break? Come into the kitchen and rest for a bit."

It would take me a few years to realize just how hard I was being on myself back then. I was on a mission to succeed, and scared to death of failure. Growing up, I'd learned that there was zero tolerance for missing the mark, so much of my behavior was driven by a desire to be perfect and avoid punishment.

When I arrived at Maryville I was like a young bird just out of the nest: I was fledging, not sure my wings could support me, but slowly learning how to fly. What I lacked in confidence I compensated for in willingness and hard work. Someone looking on from the outside would have seen a young man blessed with a good mind and a strong body, eager to learn, curious to explore new things, enchanted by psychology, savoring the process of individuation, thrilled to discover my wings worked just fine. My days were filled with classes and intramural sports, my nights with homework. My appetite for new knowledge was voracious. My efforts were rewarded with a regular spot on the dean's list. My peers elected me captain of the track team and president of our fraternity.

Once the blanket of criticism was pulled away and replaced with a quilt of acceptance, encouragement, and appreciation, I thrived. Maryville College provided the nurturing atmosphere I so desperately needed. I felt such relief to be out from under the constant criticism I'd faced at home. Each morning at Maryville I awoke eager to face the new day. Joy replaced the atmosphere of fear and dread that had surrounded me at home.

During the four years I'd be away at Maryville, I would never hear from Jule. Dad would write to me once during my senior year and put a fiver inside. That five dollars represented his total investment in my higher education. Their support and encouragement was practically nonexistent. Dad would write a few years later, toward the end of seminary, that he and Jule were viewing this as a time of allowing me to "prove myself."

From Nana, in contrast, I would receive a fistful of letters. She would enclose a dollar or two in each one. On one occasion when I wrote to thank her for the money, she cautioned me in her reply not to mention the money in any other letters going forward. “Just put a little line at the end of your letter,” she wrote, “so I know you got it.” I loved her all the more for her clandestine generosity. Words were not the only object of John’s stingy nature.

I learned how to do my own laundry that first semester at school. At times I felt a trace of envy toward some of my classmates who were sending their wash home for their moms to do, but along with doing it myself came a sense of pride that I was growing up a bit—learning to take care of myself.

Chapter 17:

Coming Into My Own

I turned twenty-one on October 2, 1953, my freshman year at Maryville. Lincoln Barker, PhD, became my next mentor. He was the cochair of the psychology department. The following year, Dr. Barker invited me to be his teaching assistant. He wanted me to coordinate the scheduling, as well as the acquisition and return of supplemental materials he used in class. Mostly these were movies produced at other colleges and universities that enriched the class by adding to what the textbook covered.

My first assignment was an experiment in learning and grace. Dr. Barker wanted a chart that showed which movie was going to be shown in which class and when that would happen. I labored away on a manual typewriter, hunting and pecking, and got all the info on a piece of paper with three carbon copies. Only by the wildest stretch of imagination could you have called it a spreadsheet.

Dr. Barker looked at it and said, "That's a good start. Now let's straighten up these columns and we'll be good to go." He praised me for what I did right, showed me what else needed to be done, and didn't belittle me for not being perfect. I couldn't believe my good luck.

The following summer I returned home and worked as a lifeguard at Holiday Lake, happy to have employment. I rode my bike from our house to the lake, a five-mile round trip. I loved working outside and soaking up the sun. A tan body seemed easier to look at than a white one; I radiated a healthy glow, one of the perks of the job. The girls adored me and I reveled in their attention.

This was before the era of sunscreen with SPF, so we slathered our bodies with Johnson & Johnson baby oil and mixed in a few drops of iodine to achieve the coveted look of a bronze god. I would not know until later that all that exposure to ultraviolet rays was damaging my skin cells, planting seeds of destruction called basal cell, squamous carcinoma, and melanoma.

The summer following my sophomore year at Maryville looked the same. I worked ten-hour days at the lake, biked home to shower, shave, and change clothes, then grabbed a bite to eat and headed for the roller rink. My hours didn't fit the meal schedule at home, so I often stopped at Charlie Hamel's Hoagie shop for a sandwich, a drink, and a package of Tastykakes.

That fall marked the beginning of my junior year at Maryville. With the required courses out of the way, I loaded up with five courses in psychology, my major. I was thriving in class, enjoying the homework, and excited to start the new semester as Dr. Barker's teaching assistant.

I returned to school in September 1956 a senior, a Big Man on Campus, and a tad more prideful than was good for me—but I was captain of the track team and president of my fraternity, and my confidence was at an all-time high.

One day while walking across campus to the psychology department, I saw the cheerleaders practicing. It was sweater season. The sun was shining. There was a chill in the air, but not enough for a coat. The chrysanthemums along the sidewalk trumpeted the season and the glorious array of colored leaves joined the symphony to announce the fall. I felt good all over. There was no emergency to attend to. I was learning not to create so many crises. I simply stood there, soaking in the warmth and beauty of the campus. I felt joy.

With a song in my heart and a bounce in my step, I paused to watch the cheerleaders. I thought to myself, *What a comely bunch—the best-looking ladies on campus.* They looked striking in their knitted white sweaters and matching pleated skirts, which were accented by the orange and garnet school colors. Those outfits accentuated their natural curves and their dance routine added some bounce to the presentation. Whether we won or lost the homecoming game, it was exhilarating to watch the cheerleaders.

I knew most of them, but there was a new one I didn't know who caught my eye. I learned from a friend that her name was Cathy Dees. She had transferred in as a sophomore and I was a senior, so we had no classes in common.

We didn't see each other again until just before Christmas break. We bumped into each other at the Student Center and talked for a while over a shake. As we talked, I discovered that she lived about twenty-five miles away from me back home. Her dad was stationed at Frankford Arsenal in North Philadelphia, just across the Delaware River from my parents' home in New Jersey.

I wrote down Cathy's address and agreed to look her up over the holidays.

My friend Bob Harding loaned me his Harley so I could go visit Cathy.

I had never been to the Arsenal before, so I felt surprised and daunted by the foreboding granite walls surrounding the place; they were cold, hard, and uninviting. The Arsenal had manufactured small-arms ammunition during the war. It was a vital source of firepower to the men on the front lines. I quickly got the message that one didn't just waltz into the place.

I felt even more intimidated by the armed guards who stopped me at the gate. Their demeanor shouted that they took their job seriously. They meant business. You'd better have a good reason for coming there. If you didn't, forget it. They called residents to make sure they were expecting visitors before admitting anybody to the base.

When they dialed Colonel Dees's number, beads of sweat formed at the small of my back. Waves of apprehension coursed through my body when they asked if he was expecting a young guy dressed in black and riding a Harley-Davidson. My mouth got dry when they asked if it was okay to admit me, and I was sweating bullets by the time he replied, "What's his name again?" *F-i-n-e-r-t-i-e*, they spelled it out for him.

When Cathy's dad said yes, I felt like a man on death row who'd just heard the news of the governor's reprieve. During the ride over the bridge I'd been hot to see her, but the screening at the gate had sure put a damper on my ardor. I felt like I was going to visit somebody in prison.

All the pomp and pride I felt in being a big man on campus at Maryville meant nothing to the guards at Frankford Arsenal. Their reception made even the bleakness at home feel warm. During this visit, I was definitely going to be on my best good-boy behavior.

Chapter 18:

Fork in the Road

Yogi Berra once humorously advised, "When you come to a fork in the road, take it." Well, while I was a senior at Maryville, I came to my own fork in the road. I had come to college as preparation for entering seminary. Early on, however, I had fallen in love with psychology. I had declared as a major in that field and had now devoured every course offered. I couldn't get enough of it. During my junior year and now during my senior year, I had continued as Dr. Barker's teaching assistant, serving as a proctor during class quizzes, grading test papers, and helping with the lab work doing experimental psychology. He was my mentor and major advisor. All the sparks of my interest centered on psychology. I didn't know what seminary was like, but I knew I loved psychology. Should

I continue on to seminary as originally planned, or go to graduate school in psychology?

I devised a test to help me figure out which fork of the road to take: why not apply to both and see what happened?

So I fired off an application to Princeton Theological Seminary and followed with another to Michigan State University for graduate study in psychology. Whoever sent the first acceptance letter would decide the issue.

In due time, I received a packet from Princeton. I jumped for joy at learning that I had been accepted. I celebrated the good news and felt relief that a decision had been made—or so I thought until, a few days later, I received a letter of acceptance from MSU.

I knew how to cope with paucity, but nothing in my life had prepared me for how to deal with abundance. This turn of events threw me right back into the angst of indecision. The sparks of excitement crackled around MSU; I was so tempted to follow my newfound love, psychology. But that course of action seemed to be a veering-off from my original call to ministry.

This set up a conflict inside my head between doing what I wanted and doing what I had been called by God to do, turning up the volume on Mom's "be a good boy" directive. The fact that Michigan was several states away tapped into my fears of getting too far away from my support system. Even though it wasn't all that great, it was all I had. I felt confident that the church would support my entrance into Princeton and serious doubt that they would endorse my dreams at Michigan State.

I'd experienced the same feeling at the top of the hill once when I was learning to ski. Until I felt some confidence in my skills, it was impossible to set out down the hill. Fear reared its ugly head and prevented me from moving forward.

Princeton was close to home. I could drive either way in thirty-five minutes. One might say about this juncture that the dragons I didn't know at Princeton were less scary than the dragons I did know at home.

The proximity of Princeton and its alignment with the original vision of my call led me to Princeton Seminary. God had provided so far; I would continue to trust him.

Summer of 1957 found me lifeguarding at Holiday Lakes again—a return to the job I had started in 1950, fresh out of high school. The previous seven years I'd worked as captain of the lifeguards. There were twenty-four of us and we worked in shifts. My job was to make sure we had adequate coverage when the lake was open to the public, and to make sure each guard got a rest break after an hour and a half on duty.

The job required a steady focus and an all-round awareness of signs of fatigue and distress in the swimmers. I'd rescued a bunch of people, and not one of them had ever cried out "help"—at least, not verbally. I had learned early on to look at their eyes and their arms. When a swimmer is in distress, his eyes get as big as saucers and his arms move in a random flapping motion that is not sustainable. Shortly afterward, he disappears beneath the water. I made sure this never happened at our lake, and I felt proud that no one had ever drowned on my watch.

This year, I returned to Holiday Lake on Memorial Day to discover that the owner had expanded the popular resort by adding a fancy Pool & Cabana Club to the property. He asked me to manage that operation.

My new position required me to collect fees for entrance to the pool and rental of the cabanas, keep the water sparkling and chemically in balance so it was inviting and safe for swimming, and manage the separate team of lifeguards we hired for the Club.

Dad had said I could live at home during that summer. This was difficult for me after having had the freedom of living in the dorm at school, where I could follow my own rules and manage my life without being subject to family restrictions, but it was worth it to me because of the money I'd save staying there.

The first hurdle I had to clear when I returned home was the loss of my room. When I brought my things into the house and went upstairs to unpack, my room was filled with my brother's things. I was furious at my parents; they hadn't saved my room for me. That was my space and they'd given it to my brother. As the firstborn, I felt seriously demoted and discounted. I felt like a displaced person. All my things were packed in boxes and stuffed in the closet. In their place were my brother's things.

Letting me come home was actually a kindness on Dad's part, though it was hard to see that at the time. Now that I was managing the Pool & Cabana Club, I was making $1.75 an hour. Even with a seventy-hour week, which was typical, my take-home pay was around a hundred dollars—not enough to support an independent existence. It was a mixed blessing, so I was thankful for the good and frustrated and angry about the bad.

When it got ugly, I left.

Chapter 19:

Between Times

Cathy and I dated some after we returned to school for the spring semester. The ethos of our school did not encourage one-on-one outings, however. The official time for dates was Tuesday evening, and this created a hardship for me, because I had four of my five classes on Wednesday. There was all that homework to do.

Guys were supposed to pick up their dates at the girls' dorm, where we waited in the parlor for them to come down from their room and sign out with the Dorm Mother. When they did so, they had to indicate where we were going and when we'd be back. After a date, couples could visit in the parlor until ten o'clock—as long as the guy kept one foot on the floor at all times.

There were not a lot of opportunities to meet up. Some couples met at "The Ruins," a designated smoking spot. But non-smokers didn't want to go there, and the fact that my roommate had gotten expelled from school for having sex there made it especially unappealing to me. Once in a while Cathy and I would slip off to the back of the chapel and get hot and bothered by reading *The Joy of Sex*, but that's as far as our physical relationship went.

I graduated in May of 1957. After that I hitchhiked to Little Rock, Arkansas, to meet Cathy's family. Her mother and aunt Hidy were living there. I wouldn't try hitchhiking today; there are so many horror stories about people who have dared to and lived to regret it. But this was a different time: the world was a kinder place. Following World War II, with its unprecedented loss and devastation, people were taking a collective sigh of relief that the conflict was over. Many veterans had returned home now and were scattered throughout the country. Some were attending college on the GI Bill. Others were looking for work or seeking a new identity and trying to discover what they might want to do with the rest of their lives. The hearts of the American people had been tenderized by the war. They wanted to express their appreciation to these courageous young men and women who had served their country, so they pulled off the highways, stopped their cars, and opened their doors to hitchhikers as a way of saying thanks.

Before leaving school, I secured permission from Mr. Curry, my RA, to store my things in the dorm for a few days. I would stop by to retrieve them on my way back from Arkansas. I put some toiletries and a change of clothes in a small bag, walked a few blocks to the highway, stuck out my thumb, held up my LITTLE ROCK sign, and waited.

It was summer, but the heat had not yet gotten unbearable. The first three cars were driven by parents of some of my classmates who were heading home. They were loaded to the headliner with college stuff and had no room for a rider. The driver of a semi-tractor and trailer slowed down as though he would stop, but he only pointed to a sign in the windshield that said "NO RIDERS" and kept going.

I had started out with a lot of hope and enthusiasm, but as the cars and trucks kept passing me without stopping, despair began to creep in. What if nobody offered me a ride? Where would I spend the night? Would I end up sleeping alongside the road? I was tired of smelling the exhaust of the cars and trucks speeding by. The dust and dirt kicked up from their tires would soon have me looking like a chimney sweep. I felt thirsty. Worse, I had that nagging feeling that it wouldn't be long before I'd need to look for a bathroom.

I sat down. I must have dozed off for a while, because I was startled by the sound of crunching gravel. A car had pulled off the highway and was approaching on the shoulder. Not just any car, either: it proudly sported the emblem of a Lincoln Continental.

The driver lowered the electric window on the passenger side. The air conditioning came out of the window and cooled my face as I leaned over so I could see him. He was dressed in a suit.

"Where you headed?" he asked.

"Little Rock."

"You're in luck," he said, "that's where I'm going. Hop in."

I would have been glad to ride in any old car or truck that came by, but now I would be riding in style. I jumped into the passenger seat without hesitation.

We drove in silence for a while. He was glad to have some company and not have to drive all those miles alone. I was relieved to be out of the heat and off the street. Before long, however, I had a serious case of goose bumps. I asked if we could back off the air conditioning.

"Sure," he said. "What's your business in Arkansas?"

I told him I had just graduated, and was on my way to meet my girlfriend and her parents in Little Rock. "How about you?" I asked.

He told me he was a traveling salesman for a large corporation on his way home from a business trip in Florida. After visiting for a while, we got comfortable with each other. My fears that he was a mobster bent on kidnapping me and his concerns about me knocking him over the head and hijacking his car subsided. He said he had left early that morning and had been driving all day. He'd be much obliged if I'd take the wheel for a while so he could catch a few z's in the backseat.

No arm-twisting needed there. We made it to Arkansas without mishap. When we arrived, I got a kick out of the fact that Cathy and her aunt both must have been wondering who was pulling up in front of their house driving a Continental!

Cathy and Carolyn's adoptive Father, Colonel Dees, who was visiting his sister Hidy in Little Rock, said I could ride with them on the way home and stopped at Maryville to pick up my things. Colonel Dees was the brother of the girls' mother and their Aunt Hidy and was in fact their Uncle Raymond.

I worked at the Pool & Cabana Club that summer and saw Cathy when I could on weekends. That September, I moved my belongings into Room 100 of Alexander Hall. I was now a "first-year student" at Princeton Seminary. That designation, like Law 1, allowed me to avoid the embarrassment of being a freshman again.

Princeton is a charming city, the scene of some of the action during the Revolutionary War. General Washington headquartered in the area with his troops and crossed the Delaware River not far from there in his surprise attack on the British troops in Trenton, a maneuver that proved to be the turning point of the war.

I was struck by the words inscribed on the gigantic marble monument to commemorate the Battle of Princeton:

Here memory lingers to recall the guiding mind,

Whose daring plan outflanked the foe and turned dismay to hope,

When Washington, with swift resolve, marched through the night,

To fight at dawn and venture all in one victorious battle for our freedom.

Princeton University also boasted the presence of The Institute of Advanced Learning on its campus. A group of the world's finest scholars lived there, taught there, and processed to dinner each evening in their academic robes and regalia. Among them had walked Albert Einstein and other Nobel laureates, great minds who, together, had tackled some of the most difficult problems we faced as human beings. I got goose bumps imagining this august body of scholars walking in formation across campus. Unfortunately, Albert Einstein died before I got there. It would have been a thrill to see him in person.

Of course, the fact that I would soon be attending this prestigious school was thrill enough on its own.

The seminary had been founded in 1812 and my dormitory was named after Lamar Alexander, the first professor to teach there. I wish I could say I was happy there, but I wasn't. The rigors of the curriculum splashed cold water on the high hopes I'd had about being in seminary. I felt depressed by the loss of the psychology courses I loved and uninspired by the challenge of learning Greek and Hebrew, church history, the English Bible, and speech. I struggled to see the diacritical marks under the Hebrew text and found no joy in the loads of assigned reading about things I didn't care about, or in watching my hair, which I did care about, fall out by the handful.

I didn't know this was a stress reaction at the time. I did know that I felt really sad and depressed about leaving behind a subject I loved and taking on classes I didn't. This change and loss hit me harder than I was willing to acknowledge. For quite some time I was in a state that would have qualified as a depressive episode. I was still functional, but I felt like I was wading through molasses up to my hips. Every step was an effort. At times I despaired at the idea of going on. I prayed, over and over, "Lord, grant me enough light to see the next step and enough strength to take it."

I'd been an honors student in college and now was on the verge of failing Hebrew and English Bible—until a visit to the local ophthalmologist and a pair of glasses helped me to see the marks I was missing.

The glasses also helped me see the strands of hair in the comb, and on the drain in the shower. After I got them, my grades improved but my morale did not. The only thing that kept me going was the conviction that, however unpleasant, this was what I was called to do—that along with occasional visits on a weekend when my friends Bob and Joyce would drive Cathy up to Princeton so we could have some time together.

I felt convinced that God had called me to ministry. It was an inner knowing that was unshakable. My job was to hear it and respond in faith. From the start I intuitively knew and trusted that this was what God really wanted for me and He would provide the guidance along the path, as well as the strength I needed to do it. This belief was reinforced, as always, by Mom's directive to be a good boy.

I feel a lot of compassion for that young man. I wish for him a mentor, or what Alice Miller calls an "enlightened witness"—someone with whom he could talk things over, someone to help him sort it out. I wish for him a healing conversation that his family's no-talk rule excluded from the realm of possibility.

Chapter 20:

A Family of My Own

I began my middle year at Princeton Seminary in fall of 1958. I continued seeing Cathy some weekends, whenever Bob and Joyce could drive her to see me. She and her twin sister, Carolyn, were still living at home at Frankford Arsenal. They were identical twins, the first I'd ever met. They looked so much alike it was a challenge to tell them apart. Once when we were together, they received a letter from their Aunt Hidy. While they were reading, they both stopped at the same moment, looked at each other, and laughed. In the beginning, the only way I could tell them apart was a nervous twitter Carolyn added at the end of her sentences.

Toward the end of that semester, Cathy broke the news that her dad was going to be reassigned to Pearl

Harbor on Oahu, Hawaii, at the end of the year. Her parents assumed that the girls would join them. Carolyn was all for it. Cathy resisted. We had grown closer during the year and a half that we had known each other. She didn't want to move overseas with her family and I didn't want her to be that far away.

We talked it over one weekend in Princeton while my roommate, Kenneth, was away visiting friends. If she stayed stateside she could find work and buy us some time to work things out. But with her parents moving away, she would have no place to stay.

"What if we get married?" I asked. "That would solve everything. You wouldn't have to move away. We could find a place to live and start our life together."

Cathy agreed. We were young, in love. This was the first serious relationship either of us had been in. We both came from seriously dysfunctional families. We both had abandonment issues. My mother had died; her father had gone missing. What could go wrong?

We were married on December 20, 1958, at the church in Delanco during Christmas break.

I think Dad and Jule liked Cathy. They thought she was good for me. They probably thought she would help to settle me down. I think Dad was also looking forward with some excitement to being a grandpa, although he never said so. (That's no surprise.) Regardless, I never felt any resistance to the marriage from them.

The seminary had no dorms for married students at the time, so we bought a twenty-eight-foot house trailer and parked it near the campus. Cathy got a job nearby at RCA as an executive secretary.

We drove a two-tone '49 Mercury at the time. It was a manual shift. Cathy took her driver's test with it at the DMV. During the road test the gear-shift lever fell out of its place on the steering column and rolled under the passenger's seat at the tester's feet. Unnerved but not completely rattled, Cathy asked if he would please hand her the stick. He did, and she replaced it on the column and completed the test.

When the test was over, Cathy was sure she hadn't passed. But when she asked him, "How did I do?" he said, "Lady, if you can drive this thing you can drive anything on the road." He handed her the test with a "PASS" stamp at the top and a reminder to have the horn fixed.

We stayed in that house trailer for a year, just enough time to conceive and bring Cathy to her third trimester with our first child. During this time we met Don and Margie Hauck, a couple we became close to and often shared dinners with over a charcoal fire in a Weber smoker. We also got a gray cat and named him Black Shadow. Images of myself at that time would continue to be a source of comfort later in life—me hunched over a textbook in that little trailer, working on an assignment for class, wearing a sweater and a scarf against the chill of a drafty trailer, Black Shadow draped around my shoulders, purring.

More and more students were coming to seminary already married, so the administration relented and acquired housing for them. In September 1959, Cathy and I got a spot in the married couples' dorm. She was growing large as her due date drew near, and we wanted to be out of that drafty trailer before our child was born.

On November 30, our first child arrived. We named her Carolyn, after Cathy's sister and Carolyn Kennedy. Our apartment was tiny—one room with a sofa and a double bed, plus a cramped kitchenette and a large walk-in closet. It wasn't much bigger than our trailer, but it wasn't drafty. Lacking other space, Carolyn slept in a crib in the closet. It was quiet both for her and for us, and the space was so tiny we could hear her if and when she cried.

We lived in this housing for nine months, until I graduated. The ceremonies were held on campus in the chapel of nearby Princeton University because Miller Chapel at the seminary wasn't big enough. Emotions rushed up into my throat as I walked across the stage to receive my diploma.

The trigger for these emotions was seeing my dad in the first row next to my uncle Ed. He had not made it to my college graduation; he had been hurt by my decision to enter the ministry. He'd tell me later that when I first shared the news of my call to ministry, it was as if I'd pointed a double-barreled shotgun at his chest and pulled the trigger. "It wouldn't have hurt me more," he'd say. In his heart he was still angry at God for taking Reeb. Now he was also angry with God for taking his firstborn son away from him—first to Maryville, then to Princeton, and later to Wyoming. In his view, God had also taken me away from his plans for me to continue the family tradition of working at Riverside Metal Company. Because of his bitterness, he had not showed up at my graduation from Maryville College.

In a letter I'd save for years, Dad wrote:

Dear Bob,

Your Ma & Pa are proud of the determination which you have shown against all odds to serve the Lord and the Church. We know of course that with God's help all things are possible. We realize now that in our efforts to make you prove yourself on your own we have not been much help. Forgive us. To you and Cathy and the child she bears on this birthday we wish you God's continued blessing, for if you have this you want for nothing. All our love, Pa.

Chapter 21:

The In-Between

Carolyn took her first breath on November 30, 1959. In May 1960, I had a diploma written in Latin that declared I was a Master of Divinity. It seemed unfair that after seven years in school, I only had a master's degree. In other professions, like medicine or law, you ended up with a doctorate after spending that much time on your studies. My awareness of this fact tarnished my trophy a bit, but overall I felt relieved that the trial by school was over, and a sense of pride at this accomplishment. If I had any suspenders I would've put my thumbs under them and crowed, "Oh, what a good boy am I. Mom would be so proud."

The downside was that I had not received a call to serve a church. Most of my classmates had, some of them well before graduation. I was all dressed up with no place to go. Uncle Ed assured me that it was just a matter of time before some church extended a call. Meanwhile, he and Aunt Mary invited us to stay at their house on the corner of Walnut and Chestnut Streets. No such invitation was extended by Jule and Dad. I found work at the Acme Markets Warehouse in Philadelphia. Acme, founded by Irish immigrants who made good in America, hired newly arrived Irish immigrants so they'd have work and be able to support themselves in their new country.

The way you got hired at Acme was by working the graveyard shift—11:00 p.m. to 7:00 a.m.—which nobody wanted. You showed up early and they selected the men they wanted to work. They picked the young and the strong. The work was backbreaking—unloading boxcars filled with all the items you could buy at Acme Market. If you put in a good night's work, the chances were good that you'd be hired again the next night. In the morning, after clocking out, you'd wait in line at the cashier's window and be paid for your labor in cash. This put some money in the pockets of new arrivals right from their first day for food and rent, and often a wee dram.

I was paired up with Ray from the beginning. We worked well together and usually unloaded at least one boxcar or "reefer" (refrigerated car) each night. Sometimes we did one and a half, depending on the contents. The reason they paired me up with an old-timer was that Ray knew how to build a pallet. We'd place each box on a pallet in a time-proven pattern so it wouldn't crumble when the forklift driver moved it from the train platform to the warehouse.

The pallets were stacked thirty feet high. Ray and I calculated one time that we each moved about sixteen foot-tons per day.

After working like that all night, I often fell asleep at the wheel of my car while waiting for the traffic light to change on my way home. I worked this job for a full year and it paid enough to provide rent and food money for Aunt Mary and Uncle Ed so we wouldn't be a drain on them.

The telephone rang in March of 1961.

"It's for you," Aunt Mary said, handing the phone to me. At the other end was DeWitt Safford, Synod Executive of the states of Wyoming and Montana. He asked if I'd be interested in serving a National Missions' church in Yoder, Wyoming. He mentioned the name of one of my seminary classmates, Griffith Matthews, who was serving at Hawk Springs, a few miles away. The rural churches were too small to support a pastor and his family on their own. The National Missions branch of the Presbyterian Church provided pastoral care for these community churches by entering into an agreement where the community would pay half and the Board of National Missions would match it.

I accepted the call. I was going to be pastor of the Yoder Community Presbyterian Church.

Before we left for Wyoming, Florence Wagner, an elder in our church, asked me to stop by her house. She had a going-away gift for me.

When I got to Florence's house, she greeted me and led the way into the den. Florence was a registered nurse. Her husband, Doc Wagner, had died a few years earlier. Doc was an avid hunter and fisherman who loved being out of doors. Florence had placed a few of his things on the sofa. First was his custom-made fly rod. It broke down into sections that could be stored in a cardboard cylinder for ease of handling and to protect them from damage. These sections fitted together with great precision and, when fully assembled, made a ten-foot pole that was a work of art. I remember thinking, *This is way too fine to take fishing.* Along with it came a box of fishing lures that Doc had tied himself.

Next Florence opened a case and produced a Winchester Model 12 twelve-gauge shotgun that Doc had used for hunting waterfowl. Their home was situated on the Delaware River, so the ducks and the geese were plentiful there.

The final prize was in a fitted wooden box lined in red velvet. When she opened the lid, I gasped. The beauty took my breath away. Inside lay a Parker Brothers 16-gauge double-barrel side-by-side shotgun. These guns are collectors' items from an era when craftsmen did most of the work by hand. The stocks were made from select burled walnut blanks fitted to the receiver and polished to a high gloss. The checkering was applied by hand. The bluing on the barrels shone like a grand piano. Master craftsmen had engraved scenes into silver panels on the receiver: a pointing dog on one side, pheasants taking flight on the other, and a covey of quail on the underside.

This was a gift fit for a king. I stood there, dumbfounded, as I realized that Florence meant to present them to me.

The sound of her voice brought me back into the room. "Since you are moving to Wyoming, I thought you could make good use of these. Doc loved them so. Since he's been gone, every time I look in our closet and see them, I cry. I'd like you to have them."

I couldn't tell if I was awake or dreaming. It seemed too good to be true. I couldn't have been any happier if I had found the Holy Grail.

Chapter 22:

Newcomers

Early in May, Cathy and I and our daughter, Carolyn, not yet two, found ourselves driving west in two cars—an Opel station wagon, and a 1950 Pontiac with a U-Haul trailing behind it—headed for my new, and first, assignment in southeastern Wyoming.

When we arrived in Yoder, Mrs. Vorpohl acted as our hostess and welcoming committee. She showed us through the church and the manse where we'd live and gave us the keys to both. The properties were adjacent to each other.

After spending a couple of days unpacking our things and getting settled in, we agreed on a time and date for Mrs. Vorpohl to drive us around the community.

We met the Smiths by accident. I am reluctant to use that word, but here's how it happened: Mrs. Vorpohl, elder and pillar of the church, was driving us around the community so we could get a sense of the lay of the land. She wanted to point out where the various members of the congregation lived. As we proceeded south out of town, she pointed to where the Splinter family lived. We turned west and passed Cecil Cooperrider's place, and then the Kirchifers'. Turning south, we saw where Harry Liske lived, and a bit further on, Henry Mulko's spread. In rural Wyoming, the ranches are big; neighbors are separated by several miles.

We turned west again and drove about four more miles before we got to the Ottos' ranch: Carl Otto to the north and his parents, who were homesteaders, on the south side of the road.

We continued another five miles west. It was snowing; the wipers squeaked as they worked to keep the windshield clean. I was on the passenger side, and Cathy and Carolyn were in the backseat. As I looked north out the window, I saw a house about a quarter of a mile back from the road, up on a hill. We drove past the house without any comment from Mrs. Vorpohl, so I asked who lived there.

"That's the Smiths," she replied. "They don't belong to the church."

It took me many years to flesh out all the meaning in that brief statement.

The snow, which had begun to fall sometime during the night, continued throughout the day. Now it was snowing in earnest; large, wet flakes blanketed the fields and turned the dirt roads to mud. The dirt in Yoder contains a lot of clay. When it gets wet, the clay gets as slick as grease. As Mrs. Vorpohl turned north to get to the next ranch, the station wagon lost traction and skidded off the road into the borrow pit.

I looked out the window and saw the surface of the road was at eye level. We were hopelessly mired down. *We're stuck*, I thought. *What do we do now?*

Then I heard it: the distinctive sound of a tractor. I cracked the window a bit so I could see. A tractor was heading in our direction. I could only guess that the driver had seen us slide off the road and he was coming to help us. It was windy outside and the earflaps on the man's cap were dancing in the breeze.

The tension in Mrs. Vorpohl's body and the expression on her face suggested that Mack Smith was the last person in the world she wanted to see. Nevertheless, she rolled down the driver's side window as he approached.

"Looks like you could use a hand," Mack said—and without further comment, he left the tractor idling, took a logging chain from the box, hooked it to the frame of the car, and pulled the car out of the ditch.

Once we were safely back up on the road, Mrs. Vorpohl introduced us, explained our mission, and thanked Mack for his help. He waved as we drove away.

I filed that act of kindness away under the heading, "What would we have done if Mack had not come along?"

It was 1961. No cell phones. No pay phones. We were eighteen miles from town. This seemed like one of those God-incidents—events that are way too complex to call an "accident."

On Friday of that week, Cathy and I were surprised by a knock on the kitchen door. When I answered, it was Mack and his wife, Ellen. They had been shopping in Torrington, the county seat, and they were stopping by to drop off some things for us.

Mack had the ruddy complexion of a rancher who spent a lot of time working outdoors. His hands silently testified to all the fences he had built and the postholes he had dug by hand, long before anyone invented an auger that could be attached to the power take-off on a tractor. His gold-rimmed glasses gave him the look of a scholar. Ellen, meanwhile, fit the picture of a pioneer woman and a rancher's wife.

They wanted to meet the new preacher and his family. They brought us some oranges and apples from town, plus a dozen eggs, some steaks, and a roast of beef from the ranch. We enjoyed a cordial visit with them and they said as they went out the door, "Come see us out at the ranch sometime. The welcome mat is out." We felt warmed by their kindness and said that we would. That visit marked the beginning of a relationship that would last for fifty-two years.

Ellen, Jim Huntley (friend), Mack

Chapter 23:

Smithpatch

On Saturday, May 13, Cathy and I accepted the Smiths' invitation to visit their ranch. The grand name was Canyon View Ranch, but most people called it Smithpatch. We packed our things into our '58 Opel station wagon, strapped Carolyn's child carrier in with the seat belt, and headed out of Yoder.

The ranch was four miles south and eight miles west of Yoder. The road was paved for about half the trip. After that we were "beyond the oil"—translation: dirt road. The sun was shining. The wind coming out of the north blew cool and took our trail of dust out over the prairie. I could see it my rearview mirror.

I was driving about twenty-five miles an hour, looking for the smoothest part of the road. The tires picked up gravel from the road and flung it against the metal wheel wells. Everything went well until I pulled up to a stop sign. The dust that had been following us caught up to us, enveloped us, and came into the car through the cracks. This unwanted intrusion triggered a bout of coughing and sneezing.

Along the way we passed wheat strips alternating between the golden stubble of last year's crop and the green of new blades pushing up through the dark patches of recently cultivated soil. We saw herds of cows—Hereford moms and their newborn calves—feeding and lying down in pastures. Groups of antelope grazed in the alfalfa fields with a couple of nice bucks among them standing aloof, protecting their harem.

I turned north at the outsized mailbox with SMITH on the side and drove toward the house. Mack had built the house himself in 1954. As I drove over the cattle guard, a pack of assorted dogs announced our arrival and ran out to greet us, among them a couple of long-eared hound dogs, a couple of mutts, and a pair of blooded blue-tick heelers. Ellen heard all the commotion and opened the screen door to come out and greet us. I would learn later that the dust cars kicked up on the road in served as an early warning system to let her know someone was coming.

"Well, hi," she said, "any trouble finding us?"

"Only a few coughs and sneezes from the dust," I replied.

"Come on in," she said, smiling. "Never mind those dogs, they make a lot of racket but they're harmless."

Looking south towards the rim

Facing north from the mailbox

Ellen wore a short-sleeved blouse and skirt, nylon stockings rolled down to her ankles, and sensible shoes. A peach-colored apron tied around her waist complemented her outfit.

She loved to cook. She spent most of her days in the kitchen preparing healthy meals. An apron was her daily uniform, a metaphor for her love and care.

"I've been fixin' some grub," she said as she beckoned us over. "We'll have supper later on." She led us up a short flight of stairs to a landing and into the kitchen. "Don't mind the mess. I keep my house clean enough to be healthy and dirty enough to be comfortable."

Whatever she was fixin' smelled wonderful. I tried to guess what it might be, but I would learn that with Ellen, you never knew. Canyon View was a working ranch. She had her husband, Mack, plus three sons and a daughter to feed. In addition there was Mack's brother Drum (short for Drummond) and a ranch hand, Jack Hamilton.

The floor was covered with pale green linoleum, functional and easy to clean. The walls were painted pastel. The table, made of solid oak, had claw-foot legs and could be extended to seat ten people by inserting extra leaves. When fully extended, it stretched into the living room, which is where Mack was when we came in.

He was seated in front of a wood desk looking through a high-powered spotting scope at something out in the pasture. When he heard us enter the room, he got up and greeted us, his gold-rimmed glasses still on

Stewart Finertie; Ellen at the sink

his head where he had propped them so they'd be out of the way.

"I've been watching that herd of antelope out there," he said, pointing beyond the large picture window.

As I followed his finger I could see across the road we had come in on to a vast prairie of grass waving in the wind—"clear to the rim," as Mack would describe it. I would learn later that the rim was two and a half miles distant. The view before us comprised about six square miles. It was a part of the Goshen Hole, a depression about thirty miles across and five hundred feet deep that was believed to have been scooped out by a glacier during the Ice Age.

"Where are they, Mack?" I asked, squinting into the distance.

"Here, take a look," he said, moving the chair he had been using so I could sit in it. "There's a good buck standing off to the right."

I peered into the reticule of the spotting scope and gasped as I saw the buck, a muscular creature with a tan and white coat topped off with an impressive set of horns. Actually, I said antlers at first, but Mack corrected me. Deer and elk have antlers made of bone, which they shed during the winter. They separate from the skull and fall to the ground. Hunters and hikers often find them where they've dropped. Antelope, in contrast, have horns, made of the same material as hair and fingernails—cellulose instead of bone. The nickname of the antelope is “pronghorn.” Their horns grow as the animal matures to match the size of its body.

“See how the flat part at the base is about the same height as his ear?” Mack said. “The curved part with a point at the end extends beyond his ear. That’s how you can tell if it’s a good buck, by how far the prong grows beyond his ear.”

I was fascinated by this majestic new creature I had never seen. I grew up in New Jersey, and the pronghorn is a creature of the western plains.

After we had taken turns watching the activity through the scope, Ellen said, “Mack, why don’t you take Bob and Cathy out for a ride to see what you can see. Carolyn can stay here and help me fix dinner.”

“You guys grab your sweaters and coats while I gas up the Jeep,” Mack said. “The weather can change quickly out here, and with the wind out of the north it could be chilly on the way back.”

After getting our things, we walked outside to find Mack. He was returning the gas hose to the pump. They had their own gas tank buried underground and a pump to keep all the work vehicles running and to save a lot of trips to town, which was eighteen miles away. The Jeep was silver, a commercial model with four-wheel drive, no top, and a roll-bar behind the front seat.

Mack put a gallon jug of water in the back, along with a couple of long-handled spades. He picked-up on my quizzical look and said, “In case we come across a rattler or get stuck." A bolt-action high-powered rifle also rested in a leather scabbard between the front seats—"in case we see a coyote."

It was one thirty when Mack placed a paper sack on the floor behind the driver's seat and we all hopped in. I was riding shotgun as we headed out of the yard and proceeded down the driveway. When we got to the road we'd come in on, Mack turned right and headed west out into the pasture. One mile later, I learned to open my first wire gate.

The pastures were all fenced with barbed wire to keep the cows in. Gates were placed at the corners for extra strength and to allow people and vehicles to move between pastures. The dust followed behind us like a contrail on a plane and glazed us over with a layer of fine powder. The gates were held closed by two loops of wire at the top and bottom of the post. Pushing the top of the gate post toward the corner post created a little gap so I could slip the retaining wire over the top of the post. By lifting the post out of the wire loop at the bottom, the gate came free. I then walked it into the pasture I was entering until there was enough room to allow the vehicle to pass. Once the Jeep had passed, I returned the post to the bottom loop, pushed it toward the corner post, and slipped the top loop back over the post.

I considered leaving the gate open to save work on the way back, but Mack reminded me kindly—but firmly—of the law of the range: "If the gate's shut when you get there, leave it shut; if it's open, leave it open. That's the way the rancher wants it. Besides," he added, "we may not come back this way."

I hadn't thought of that.

Mack grinned as I returned to the Jeep and climbed in. "Now you know why I like to bring somebody along when I check the windmills."

I looked at the broad pastures and the big sky stretched out before us and replied, "Opening and closing a few gates is a small price to pay for all this grandeur."

Mack drove in silence for a while on the tracks that wended their way through the pasture. He kept scanning the horizon as though he were looking for something. I looked down at his hand on the steering wheel, tanned from working in the sun, gnarled from digging postholes for miles of fences, knuckles enlarged by a touch of arthritis (which, he said, he treated each day with a tablespoon of cherry juice and vinegar). I couldn't help comparing his hand to mine: his calloused and roughened from riding and roping and slinging bales of hay, mine smooth and soft from reading, writing, and preparing sermons. I felt a twinge of envy. Each of us was searching for the Creator, but somehow his quest seemed easier in the midst of all this natural wonder.

"There they are." Mack's comment startled me out of my reverie. He stopped the Jeep and grabbed his binoculars off the dashboard to take a closer look. I looked in the direction he was glassing. A herd of antelopes stood looking at us from a quarter mile away, barely visible except for the way the afternoon sun reflected off their white rumps.

"Let's see if we can get a closer look," he said, already turning the key in the ignition. We left the tracks and headed across the pasture and into a draw where the antelope couldn't see us. Mack knew this land like the back of his hand. His father, George, had homesteaded here. Mack and his brother Drum had covered the ranch countless times on horseback, rounding up cows, mending fences, and running off predators. He knew how to sneak up on game so we could get a closer look. We drove up that wadi for some time, what I judged to be six hundred yards, until we came to a place where we could climb out. He shifted into four-wheel drive—low range, so we could make the grade.

He had judged his distance well. When we came up over the hill a herd of twenty-eight pronghorns stood in front of us, about eighty yards away. My heart leaped up in my throat at this encounter. I had never seen these majestic creatures so close. I could feel the pounding in my chest, hear the throbbing in my temples, and see my pulse as I glassed them with my binoculars.

They stood there, ears twitching, legs growing restless, studying us for a few seconds, trying to assess the danger. The dominant buck must have winded us. He snorted and turned and led them out of danger. They can put a lot of distance between you in a hurry at up to forty miles an hour.

"Wow," I said.

Mack grinned. "They're great surveyors, too. Once they go over a hill they follow the natural valleys and keep on running. The next time you see them they'll be a quarter mile away. Today they were pretty quiet and curious. In the fall, during hunting season, they get really spooky. You can glass them for a while from inside the vehicle, but as soon as you crack a door they'll be gone."

Mack drove a big loop around the ranch. He studied the cattle with a knowing eye, making sure they were okay. We stopped at a windmill to make sure they had enough water, and paused to take a drink ourselves. The water ran clear and cool into the tank. Mack took a tin can from the top of a fencepost, leaned over the tank, filled it from the spout, and handed it to me.

"Try this," he said, "it's the best well on the place except the one at the house."

I would learn later that Mack or his dad had drilled every well on the ranch using a surplus army halftrack with a drill rig he put on it. His son, Jerry, had the gift of dowsing with a stick. He had shown them where to drill using this gift with amazing accuracy.

Meadowlarks flew up out of the grass with their brilliant yellow bodies and distinctive voice. Sagebrush crackled under the weight of the tires as we drove cross country, and that aromatic smell of sage offered a welcome respite from the dust, as though the spirits of the Indians were riding with us and squeezing their atomizer bulbs from time to time. I reveled in the bigness of the sky, the ability to see for miles, the wind in our faces, and the freshness of the sagebrush scent in my nose as we rambled across the prairie. It's as close to heaven as I've ever been. Today, the smell of sage still transports me back to Wyoming in a jiffy.

At the next gate Mack turned left and we headed north toward the ranch house. As we turned, a coyote loped across the pasture three hundred yards in front of us. Most of the country is dry, but at one point we crossed a small stream produced by a spring flowing out of the rim rock. A stand of cottonwood trees grew there, a sure sign that there was water.

Mack downshifted the Jeep in order to get more traction in the mud. To the left of those cottonwoods, he pointed to a group of mule deer. Larger of body and darker than the antelope, they too had cream-colored fannies. They sported large forked antlers rather than horns.

Instead of running like a horse or a dog, mule deer take bounding leaps up to twenty feet at a time using all four hooves at once. When they come to a fence, they bound over it like a high jumper at a track meet. Antelope slow down and go between the wires.

Climbing in and out of the Jeep to open and close the gates produced in me a feeling of satisfaction that I had done something useful that day. As a pastor, it was not as easy to see what I had accomplished some days. As we drew closer to the house, I savored the pleasant feeling of tiredness that accompanies useful work, along with some pangs of hunger. Bouncing across the pastures out in the fresh air had worked up my appetite.

The last gate was open. I hadn't noticed that. As I made a move to get out of the Jeep, Mack grinned and said, "I'll get this one."

Got me. I grew to love this pioneer cowboy with his wry sense of humor and accepting ways. He was so different from my dad, in ways that I hungered for.

As we passed the mailbox and headed up the driveway, the dogs welcomed us and sniffed the Jeep to determine where we'd been and what we'd been up to. Mack drove into the garage and parked. We piled out of the Jeep and headed for the house.

Ellen had been busy while we were away. The aromas of supper welcomed us into the house. We climbed the steps up to the landing and paused at the double sink to wash off the dust of the journey.

"I fixed some grub," Ellen said. "Find yourselves a place to sit and help yourselves. Mack sits on that end and I sit on this one so I'll be close to the kitchen."

The table would have groaned if it could have under the weight of the steaming dishes loaded on it. A large platter of meat occupied the center. It could have been beef, buffalo, elk, antelope, or venison—I would learn quickly that you didn't ask, you just took some and enjoyed it. There were mashed potatoes with a tureen of piping-hot gravy to smother them with, green beans,

Mack and Bob

Back row: Mack (seated), Wiedenhafts (friends) at piano, Royce Smith

Front row: Pat Smith (kneeling), unknown, Cathy with Stewart, Carolyn, Ellen, Stan Smith

and corn from last year's garden, Ellen's special cucumber salad, freshly baked bread, home-churned butter, honey, and chokecherry jelly made of berries she'd picked in the canyon. A veritable feast fit for a king, like Thanksgiving in May.

Ellen took great pride in her cooking and satisfaction knowing that everything on the table was grown in her garden or out in the pasture. We all stuffed ourselves until we were "as full as a tick" then retired to the basement to shoot some pool. Their eldest son, Jerry, excused himself to get cleaned up for a date and then headed out in his brand-new, fire-engine-red Ford convertible.

He hadn't been gone long when we heard the back door close. It was Jerry.

"That was a quick date," Mack said.

"Never got there," Jerry said. "Couldn't make it up the hill going north; too slick."

Hearing this, Mack suggested we stay with them overnight. No point in taking a chance. If Jerry couldn't make it, neither could we.

Anxiety tied my guts in knots as reality began to sink in. Here I was, stranded eighteen miles from town on the eve of preaching my first sermon at my new church. I had no sermon ready, and all my books and resources to help craft one were miles away.

My custom was to read all week in preparation, then get up at 4:00 a.m. to write the sermon. I'd finish around eight o'clock, go next door to rehearse it from the pulpit, return home to have breakfast, shower, shave, and dress in time for first Sunday school at nine forty-five, and then worship at eleven.

The snow foiled that plan. Sleep came in snatches that night. Snow fell steadily.

On Mother's Day, May 14, 1961, we awoke to find fourteen inches on the ground. Spring snows are wet, and with no wind the flakes had piled up on the power lines until the sheer weight of it broke the wires. After breakfast, Mack jumped into a military surplus half-track with a snow plow in front and cleared the way for us to get back to town.

It was eight miles from Smithpatch to the oil. As we followed Mack, we noticed that every telephone pole we passed had snapped in two. The top sections with the cross pieces were all lying in the snow; pieces of freshly splintered wood pointed toward the sky. Mack explained later that once the wire broke, the sudden loss of tension caused the poles in both directions to snap like a row of dominoes.

We made it to town fairly quickly, but there wasn't time to write a new sermon. I fished in my files for an old one that might be relevant and smiled with relief when I came across "Sweet Are the Uses of Adversity."

Shakespeare to the rescue.

Chapter 24:

Connections

New pastor, new church; a lot of firsts happened there. First death, first funeral, first Baptism, first wedding, first time appearing in court to try to support both families in a bitter suit over an accident where two teenagers had died. Hoping not to alienate either family by sitting on one side or the other, I stood in the back of the courtroom.

June 1961. It was time to meet some of my sheep, so I packed a tuna sandwich, an apple, and some lemonade and headed west out of Yoder. Hopeful that the Spirit would lead me, I drove for a while, keeping my eyes open. My heart raced at the sight of a flock of Canada geese out in the alfalfa and a big buck antelope on the wheat strips.

Then I saw a man on a combine. He was at the far end of the field, so I parked off the road to wait for him.

He pulled up next to me in a cloud of dust and wheat chaff. He climbed down off the combine and walked over to greet me.

I reached for his extended hand. “Bob Finertie; I’m your new pastor.”

“O Revender, Clyde Yeik, I been hearin’ about you. What brings you out this way?”

“I want to meet some of the people.”

“Hmm.”

“That job looks hot and dusty,” I said, lifting my Thermos. “How’s a swallow of lemonade sound?”

He nodded. “Sounds good.”

I opened the Thermos and poured some into the cup. He drank it hungrily and smacked his lips with a satisfied exhalation. “That sure hit the spot.”

“Want more?” I asked.

“No, that’ll do.” He handed the cup back to me.

“I’ve never ridden on a combine like that. Could I ride a couple of rounds with you, Clyde?”

He looked skeptical. “Oh Revender, you’d get all covered in dust and chaff.”

“I reckon it’ll wash off of me the same as it washes off of you,” I said with a chuckle.

He hadn’t thought of that. “Well, if you’re sure, hop on.”

I did. Clyde was right: it was hot and dusty and hard to breathe. But I had the time of my life riding around with him, tasting what it was like to harvest wheat.

I drove away from that encounter shaking my head

in amazement at how a small act of kindness can turn two strangers into friends.

A working ranch in Wyoming is a no-frills place. The men work hard all day and come home hungry. Because of this, Ellen spent most of her time in the kitchen preparing meals. She took pride in raising the food they ate in the large garden in back of the ranch house. She planted tomatoes, cucumbers, squash, rhubarb, string beans, carrots, watermelons, and corn. The excess food she grew during the season she put up in Mason jars.

Mack enjoyed taking guests down the cellar steps to brag on how "lazy" his wife was. He'd fling open the door to the pantry to reveal the shelves sagging under the weight of the jars of fruit and vegetables she had canned, all from her garden, and Ellen would bask in the joy of being able to do this for her family.

In addition to the vegetables, she planted flowers all around the perimeter of the house and in two beds at the gate on both sides of the sidewalk leading up to the house. She loved having guests from outside the state and other countries. Her sister, Nelly, operated an exchange student program each summer where high school students could visit the United States for two weeks. She'd drive them up from Greely, Colorado in a van to visit Smithpatch to make a tour of the ranch and enjoy some of Ellen's cooking. At the end of their visit, Ellen would give each one a plastic bag with a sprig of sagebrush, an expired Wyoming license plate with a cowboy riding a bucking bronco, and a button from a rattlesnake, and savor the oohs and aahs these unusual going-away presents unleashed.

After graduating from Normal School, Ellen had taught school in a one-room schoolhouse. In years to come while attending school reunions, former students would still refer to her as Miss Otto, her maiden name, and she'd know they belonged to that era before she was married.

Ellen loved children and enjoyed having them around the house. One afternoon we returned to the house after an excursion with Mack looking for Indian arrowheads. Because of all the game in the area, it was a favorite hunting ground. Sometimes after a big blow, the wind would rearrange the soil and uncover an arrow point. If you walked around a bit and kept your eyes open, you might get lucky and find one. I still have a couple of prized points I found during one of those expeditions.

When we came back to the house, I was surprised to see a gate installed at the top of the landing. It turned out that Ellen was babysitting some of her "grands" and wanted to keep them safe.

I let out an audible gasp as I entered the kitchen. Every cabinet door was flung open. All the pots and pans were strewn across the linoleum floor. Our daughter, Carolyn, and two of Ellen's grands were banging away on overturned pots with wooden spoons. Another was dropping wooden clothespins into the mouth of a glass milk bottle.

"It improves their hand-eye coordination," Ellen said, totally oblivious to all the mayhem.

It was way too much of a mess for that part of me that craves order.

Mack worked hard for everything he had: the land, the ranch house, the cows, and the cabin. Yet he didn't think of himself as the owner. He saw himself more as a trustee whose calling was to take care of what had been given him and to share it with others. I find that refreshing in a time of overinflated egos.

Smithpatch was a natural hunting ground, as the Indians had known for centuries before the Smiths arrived. Mack was generous. If someone stopped at the house and asked for permission to hunt, he'd send them to a section of the ranch reserved for that purpose. But if anybody tried to sneak onto the property and hunt without permission, he'd run them off the place in a heartbeat.

Chapter 25:

My Favorite Place

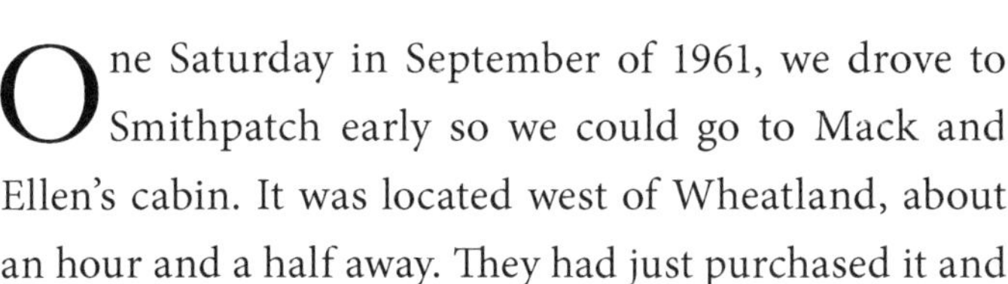

One Saturday in September of 1961, we drove to Smithpatch early so we could go to Mack and Ellen's cabin. It was located west of Wheatland, about an hour and a half away. They had just purchased it and wanted us to see it.

We all piled into the Land Cruiser and headed west up over the rim and past the wheat strips up on top. As we passed the grain elevator at Chugwater, Mack told us the town had gotten its name from the chuffing sound the bison made as they were driven over the edge of a cliff and plunged into the water below during the Indian hunt.

We skirted the city of Wheatland and kept driving west toward Laramie Peak. At 10,272 feet, this mountain was visible from the ranch.

In order to get to the cabin, we had to pass through a piece of land owned by the True Oil Company. Mack had an agreement with True that he could drive through their land. This was prime hunting country, so True had hired a guy named Glen Hall to guard the entrance and keep other people off their land. Glen lived in a house trailer by the gate.

A ritual governed what happened next. We drove up to the trailer and climbed out of the Land Cruiser to say hi to Glenn. Nobody home. We were there only a few minutes when Glen appeared on a speckled roan with his faithful dog, Shep, alongside him.

"Wondered where you were," Mack said.

"Checkin' on the cows up yonder," Glen replied.

"We brought you a little somethin'," Mack said. (He meant a bottle of blackberry brandy and a roll of Skoal.)

"Appreciate it," Glen said.

Glen remained on his horse during our visit. He was a frontier cowboy with spurs, chaps, work-worn jeans, and a ten-gallon hat with a sweat band that gave mute evidence of years of hard work in the sun.

Glen pulled out a pouch of tobacco and a paper and began to roll a smoke.

Jack Hamilton broke the silence. "That dog of yours ever chase deer?"

Glen took in the question as he licked the paper to seal the roll. He drew a wooden match out of his vest pocket and struck it on his saddle, lit the cigarette, took a deep drag, and blew out the match as he answered, "Not more than once, he wouldn't."

After giving that a few moments to sink in, Mack said, "We'll be on our way."

"If you catch any fish while you're up there," Glen said, "I'd be glad to have a change in my diet. A fella gets kinda tired eatin' venison all year."

"You bet."

We drove through the True ranch and made our way toward the cabin. The last stretch was rough going. Mack had to shift into four-wheel drive to make the grades at times, and the rocky road was passable only with a vehicle like the Land Cruiser with its high clearance.

As we cleared the last hill and came around a bend, the cabin came into view on the other side of a stream. Mack pulled up as though he were going to drive across it, then stopped. Normally the North Laramie River was crossable with a four-wheel drive, but recent showers had swollen the stream to a level where it was impassable. Mack found a place to park and we all climbed out to have a look.

"Since we can't drive across, we'll have to try something else," Mack said. He pointed to a nearby tree. He had strung a heavy cable across the river, from the tree near us to one on the other side. He had welded a cable car in his shop and put some pulleys on it so it could ride on the cable. This allowed two people at a time, plus their gear, to pull themselves across the river by means of a rope attached to the other side.

We went over two by two until everybody was on the other side, and nobody had to get wet.

After fixing a picnic lunch, we spent the afternoon exploring the area around the cabin. A granite cliff about a thousand feet high rose up behind the cabin.

We found a game trail and followed it up to the top, where we stood in awe of the view. It was here that I discovered my favorite place, and this poem bubbled up:

A granite saddle with a jaw-dropping view

Up by Laramie Peak, in southeastern Wyoming,

Not far from Chugwater and Hubbards' Cupboard.

High above the cabin where I'm staying, and
The North Laramie River that gurgles as it flows
beside it.

As I sat down, I noted the multicolored lichen
growing on the rock;

It now forms a rude cushion between the granite
and me.

I look UP and see the kaleidoscopic patterns of the clouds,

Always moving, shifting, changing.

The sky is a cosmic Etch A Sketch

On which the Creator forms a cloudscape,

Then raises up a breeze to clear it all away,

Only to begin again.

I look DOWN: and see the sculptured carpet of evergreens

That covers the floor of the valley as far as my eye can see;

Mostly lodge pole pines, with a few ponderosas sprinkled in;

And here and there, splashes of shimmering gold that mark the aspen groves;

As though the Creator were a French Impressionist.

I look AROUND: and marvel at the variety of wildlife;

From the eleven-hundred-pound bull elk

With his massive antlers laid back

To streamline him as he glides through the forest;

To the four-and-a-half-ounce chipmunk,

Scampering across the needles on the forest floor.

I look WITHIN: I'm filled with awe

By the majesty of creation;

Stunned by the thought that all this

Has been provided for our enjoyment and sustenance.

I breathe deeply as I try to take it all in.

As I do, I am inspired,

But most of all I am at peace,

Here in my favorite place.

Chapter 26:

Learning to Stay

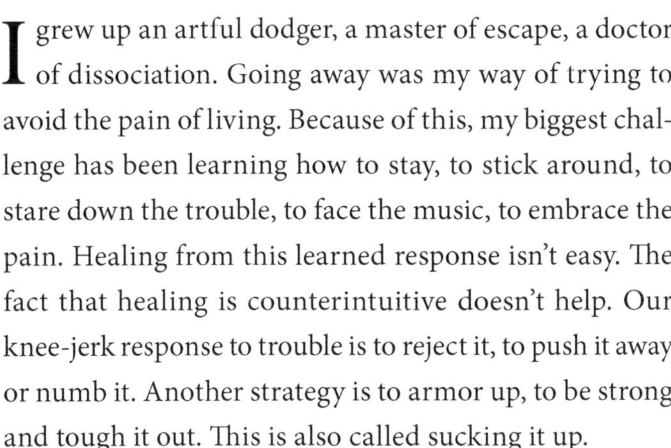

I grew up an artful dodger, a master of escape, a doctor of dissociation. Going away was my way of trying to avoid the pain of living. Because of this, my biggest challenge has been learning how to stay, to stick around, to stare down the trouble, to face the music, to embrace the pain. Healing from this learned response isn't easy. The fact that healing is counterintuitive doesn't help. Our knee-jerk response to trouble is to reject it, to push it away or numb it. Another strategy is to armor up, to be strong and tough it out. This is also called sucking it up.

Some people turn to alcohol to ease the pain. It's readily available and doesn't require a prescription. Visit any bar or club at happy hour; all the drinks are two-for-one, so in no time you're feeling no pain. What's not obvious in the beginning, however, is that the body learns to tolerate alcohol. Over time it takes more and more to achieve the desired effect. At some point you realize that you could drink Canada dry and still have the pain when sober. And now you're also dealing with addiction.

The trouble with being tough is, you can't be tough forever. What then? What if the key that unlocks the pain is surrender? What if instead of putting up your dukes, you drop them at your side—or fold them in prayer? What if you don't run away? What if you decide to stay?

One of the things I wanted to do before I die, an item near the top of my bucket list, was to take a trip down through the Grand Canyon on the Colorado River. One year, I purchased a travel guidebook so I could read about it.

There were two options available:

1) you could go in a large inflatable rubber raft, or

2) you could go in a wooden dory.

The author compared the raft trip to going down the river in a bus, while riding in a dory was like going down the river in a Porsche. Since I am an adrenaline junkie, I chose the dory.

When the boatman pushed off from the beach at Phantom Ranch, the river was quiet. In those first few miles, he briefed us on what to expect when we hit our first rapid.

Rapids form where the canyon narrows and the elevation drops. The same volume of water has to squeeze through a narrower opening in the riverbed, so it speeds up as it passes through. This is called the Venturi effect. In addition, gravity causes the water to accelerate as it moves downhill. Often nature will place a curve at the bottom of a rapid and a sheer rock wall. From inside the boat, it looks like you're going to crash into the wall—but you don't, because all that water caroms off the wall and forms a giant wave that comes at the bow of the boat at a 45-degree angle.

What happens next is critical. Seeing that wave about to crash over the boat and realizing that the temperature of that water is 54 degrees Fahrenheit, the people on the wave side instinctively want to avoid that frigid bath. If they do, everybody ends up in the river. What they must do instead is totally counterintuitive. They must do the last thing they want to do. It's called a "high-side maneuver": they must lean into that wall of water and allow it to crash over them. They will be thoroughly chilled and the boat will take on a lot of water, but the boat will remain upright and proceed down the river. Then everybody has to bail the water out, because the boatman doesn't have much control over a dory that's full of water.

I think this story serves as an excellent metaphor for life. What if I decide to execute my own high-side maneuver? What if I choose not to run away? What if I decide to stay?

Epilogue

Growing up in an alcoholic family system, I swallowed the unspoken rules: *Don't talk. Don't trust. Don't feel.* Relationships are challenging when these rules are in place. Add to that a default defense mechanism of dissociation (going away when the pain threatens to overwhelm) and the result is a detached, distant, and lonely life. It's no surprise, then, that when times got tough, my marriage to Cathy didn't last. I went away—physically, emotionally, and sexually—and because of that, we were divorced in 1971.

I remarried in 1974, this time to Lynn. We were together for seven years, and I went away again. We divorced in 1981.

I married Diana on the rebound. That relationship didn't last a year. Wounded and hurting deeply, I resolved to stay single until I could sort out some of my issues and gain some healing. I needed time to recover from sexual addiction and a penchant for dissociation.

I faithfully attended Adult Children of Alcoholics and Codependency groups for seven years to gain some recovery. In addition, I participated in a therapy group once a week.

In 1987, I met Leslie in the ACOA program. We married in June of 1988. I enrolled in graduate school at St. Mary's University in San Antonio and graduated with a master's degree in Marriage and Family Therapy in 1990. We agreed that we wanted to start a family and that the time was right. After a heartbreaking stillbirth during the initial pregnancy, we plucked up our courage and agreed to try again.

At twelve weeks in, we went to the doctor's office for a sonogram. Anxiety mounted in each of us during the drive to his office. This time there was life; not one heartbeat but two. We were going to have twins. Leslie had had a dream the previous night that we were walking through a meadow hand in hand and each of us had a child's hand in the other.

This radical news triggered my default response to stress. A voice in my head started screaming, "I want out of here."

I recognized this moment as a turning point in my life. This time I was going to try something different. I was going to say "no" to that voice. I was going to stay.

I couldn't talk about it then, but recently, in an attempt to be more open and vulnerable, I shared that story with Leslie. She saw the tears in my eyes and matched them with her own. "I'm so glad you stayed," she told me.

"So am I," I said. "It's the best decision of my life."

We celebrated our thirtieth anniversary in June.

Acknowledgments

Although *writing* a book is a solitary experience, *publishing* a book is not. Like producing a play, it takes a cast of characters. I'd like to thank them here.

Brooke Warner and Linda Joy Myers. I caught the memoir bug from you. You got me started with your online classes. You taught me the craft of memoir. Your excitement about the genre rubbed off on me.

Thanks Brooke, for your constancy. I have been a beneficiary of your encouragement, your grace, and your consummate editorial acumen.

Thanks Linda Joy, for your "keep writing" mantra, your group coaching sessions, and your own memoirs.

Ruth Stender, fellow author and friend, whose intuitive insights blessed me along the way.

Tabitha Lahr, who created the cover and made the inside look great.

Krissa Lagos and Chris Dumas, your suggestions enriched the text and your proofreading made it flow.

Becky Garza, my daughter, who laughed and cried with me as I wrote and gave me feedback about the parts that touched her heart and those that didn't.

Terry and Gary, the other two legs of our triad, thanks for listening.

Thursday night men's Bible study group, thanks for asking "When is it going to be done?" It's done.

The people who populated Smithpatch—Mack and Ellen, Jerry, Stan, Royce and Pat—who found room in their hearts to love me. All those years I thought I was driving to Yoder to hunt mule deer and antelope. Now I understand why my eyes filled with tears each year when I crossed the cattle guard and the house came into view. They were tears of joy. I was coming home.

Carl Grant, enlightened witness and spiritual guide during the journey.

Mark Matousek, you helped me look in the shadows at wounds I didn't want to see, allowing me to heal them.

Leslie, my wife, whom I treasure. You make our house a home and allow space for me to write. Without you this book never would have seen the light of day.

About the Author

Bob Finertie was born in New Jersey, the Garden State, and now lives in California, the Golden State. Bob writes to live and lives to write. His favorite authors are Herman Melville and Cheryl Strayed. His other passion is nature photography. When his kids' kids started having kids, he knew it was time to write this book. His goal in this book is to connect with people.

Connect with him at rwfinn@comcast.net.

Made in United States
Orlando, FL
31 January 2023

29282789R00114